Viswanathan Anand, known fondly as Vishy, is one of the most prominent names in chess. Over the three decades since he turned Grandmaster, he has won five World Championship titles among innumerable other tournaments and has continued to push past barriers to remain among the world's top chess players. His achievements have helped inspire a generation of chess players in India. Vishy is an astronomy buff, and an avid reader on maths, economics and current affairs. He loves to travel, and particularly enjoys wildlife safaris. He supports many charitable causes, chief among them being that of children with cerebral palsy and other neurological disabilities.

Susan Ninan is a sports writer with ESPN and is based in Bengaluru. She has previously worked with the *Times of India*, and has covered major sporting events like the Commonwealth Games and the World Chess Championships. When she is not writing on sport or travelling to find a story, she loves sniffing around bookstores and going backpacking, or at best making plans for the latter.

Praise for the book

'I felt very engaged while reading *Mind Master*. It was almost like chatting with Anand, but at the same time rather than hearing a great champion I saw a very natural, wise and vulnerable man. Writing a deep book is a great accomplishment… My wholehearted congratulations!' – Levon Aronian, chess Grand Master

'*Mind Master*, in chess terms, is a novelty…a whiff of fresh air. It borders on a novel (Anand probably wanted it to read like that) with his life experiences and contains traces of an invisible writer, especially when he talks of himself as the "other". A collection of moments from his career and life, both serious and silly, which blend into one whole.' – *Open*

'Wonderfully captures the drama and intrigue that can surround chess.' – *Firstpost*

'Several things raise this book well above the norm in terms of sporting biographies. There are other stellar qualities as well. The narrative dips in and out of Anand's life, pausing to take snapshots of key moments. Somehow, without going through the tedium of chronological description, it gives a pretty complete picture of his life and career…and utterly fascinating descriptions of Anand's thought processes.' – *Business Standard*

'Many moments in…*Mind Master: Winning Lessons from a Champion's Life*…will surprise you. "We didn't know that about him!" plays out like a refrain in your mind as the five-time World Champion takes you through his phenomenal journey, the highs and the lows of being a champion.' – *Telegraph*

'This is one of those books which you do not want to finish early, you want to savour every essence of it and then reminisce the pleasant as well as some unpleasant memories to treasure all the highs and lows that Vishy Anand went through in his life.' – *ChessBase*

'The book will not only appeal to chess aficionados and sports fans, but can also become a template for any youngster trying to chart out a life path which is somewhat different from the norm.' – *Financial Express*

'In [*Mind Master*], Viswanathan Anand offers golden words of advice on how young players should make their moves in the competitive world of chess… [The] milestones and roadblocks in a champion's journey are effectively explained.' – *Sunday Mid-Day*

MIND MASTER

MASTER

Winning Lessons from a Champion's Life

VISWANATHAN ANAND

with
Susan Ninan

hachette
INDIA

First published in hardback in India in 2019 by Hachette India
(Registered name: Hachette Book Publishing India Pvt. Ltd)
An Hachette UK company
www.hachetteindia.com

This edition published in 2022

6

Copyright © 2019, 2022 Viswanathan Anand

Viswanathan Anand asserts the moral right to be identified
as the author of this work.

All rights reserved. No part of the publication may be reproduced, stored in a retrieval system (including but not limited to computers, disks, external drives, electronic or digital devices, e-readers, websites), or transmitted in any form or by any means (including but not limited to cyclostyling, photocopying, docutech or other reprographic reproductions, mechanical, recording, electronic, digital versions) without the prior written permission of the publisher, nor be otherwise circulated in any form of binding or cover other than that in which it is published and without a similar condition being imposed on the subsequent purchaser.

The views and opinions provided in this book are the author's own and the facts are as reported by him and have been verified to the extent possible. The publishers are not in any way liable for the same.

Images in photo insert on pp 17, 18 (top), 19, 20, 21 and 22 courtesy Eric van Reem; on p. 18 (bottom) © New in Chess; on p. 23 © Lennart Ootes. The remaining images are from the private collections of Elizbar Ubilava, Frederic Friedel and Viswanathan Anand.

Hardback edition ISBN 978-93-5195-150-6
Paperback edition ISBN 978-93-91028-21-3
Ebook edition ISBN 978-93-5195-151-3

Hachette Book Publishing India Pvt. Ltd
4th/5th Floors, Corporate Centre,
Plot No. 94, Sector 44, Gurugram – 122003, India

Typeset in Charter BT 10.5/16
by InoSoft Systems, Noida

Printed and bound in India
by Manipal Technologies Limited

MIX
Paper | Supporting
responsible forestry
FSC
www.fsc.org FSC™ C043100

For my mother, who told me to always write down my thoughts, good or bad. She said, 'One day you will read them and realize how beautiful they are.'

'Regrets, I've had a few
But then again, too few to mention
I did what I had to do
And saw it through without exemption.
I planned each charted course
Each careful step along the byway…
Yes, there were times, I'm sure you knew
When I bit off more than I could chew
But through it all, when there was doubt
I ate it up and spit it out
I faced it all and I stood tall
And did it my way…'

'My Way', Lyrics by Paul Anka
Sung by Frank Sinatra in 1969

CONTENTS

1   DITCHING THE LADDER   5
Of Gut, Heart and a Winning Idea

2   STICKY NOTES   19
Madras, Manila, Madrid and Everything in Between

3   THE ART OF REMEMBERING   39
Hooks, Hacks and Serendipity

4   WIN SOME, LOSE SOME   57
Emotions and the Power of Objectivity

5   GATHERING THE TROOPS   77
How to Make Preparation Count and Tactics Work

6   NEW YORK, NEW YORK   99
The Making of a Champion

7   THE GIFT AND THE GRIT   121
Making Talent Work Hard

8   MINING THE MIND AND MACHINES   137
Decision-Making, Data and a New Giant on the Block

9   BONN AGAIN   165
Finding Beauty in Risk

10   THE ADVERSITY ADVANTAGE   183
A Volcanic Ash Cloud, a Road Trip and a Title

Contents

11   TWO CITIES, ONE STATE   213
Battling Learned Helplessness

12   STAYING ALIVE   241
On Today's Wins and Tomorrow's Horizons

13   PAUSE, REBOOT   261
Learnings from a Pandemic and New Beginnings

Acknowledgements   289

BONN, 2008.

My heart thumps in my ears. My fingernails mock me; over the next few hours, they could be ravaged. A World Championship match can transform its protagonists. You are never the same after it.

My wife, Aruna, manages a benign smile as we wait, wordless and anxious, to leave for the game. It's the worst time for small talk. I search my mind for a tune to hum, but the nervous energy gushing through me dismisses the idle thought.

I feel Aruna's hand on mine. It's what the subarctic tundra must feel like. Time to go, she gestures. I give her a half-kiss and she responds with the customary, 'All the best, ma.'

As the car zips out of the driveway, it hits me like shrapnel: This is the point of no return. My brain struggles to piece together what now appears at best like a cloudy preparation memory. Seated to my right, Aruna watches me, sees my hands tremble and holds them in a tight clasp.

'I need to speak to Radek,' I hear myself say. 'I can't recall a thing.' Radoslaw Wojtaszek, Radek, is one of my four trainers for the match. At 21, he's the youngest member in the team.

Aruna grapples with the two chunky mobile phones she's holding, picks one up and dials at a feverish pace. We wait in silence for a voice to come to life at the other end. The phone rings itself out. We look at each other. She tries a second time. Still no answer.

'Try the others,' I offer, surprised that I still have some dregs of pragmatism left in me. The three pale-blue-and-silver inclined cones of the Bonn Federal Art Gallery, the match venue, now tower ahead of us. Aruna asks the driver to park a few metres away, thumbs through the contact list on the phone and dials the numbers of the three remaining members of my team – Peter Heine Nielsen, Rustam Kasimdzhanov and Surya Sekhar Ganguly. No one answers. All we hear is the dull ringing and our hearts pounding. I chide myself for scouring for omens, and yet I can't help but think they weirdly have a way of proving their efficacy.

Oblivious to the doom and gloom behind him, the driver turns on the ignition and pulls up at the gallery with a gentle screech. Aruna climbs out. I stay put, undecided. She throws a mild reprimand my way, '*Onnum pannamudiyathu, ma... Poi velaiyadu.* There's nothing that can be done now... Go, play.' On a regular day, the counsel may well have ended in a marital squabble. Today, I know she has a point.

We reach the revolving door of the theatre. It's locked. We manage a pale smile at each other and wonder why the gods are against us. Someone tries to force open the iron door nearby, but it won't budge.

'Use the other entrance,' Aruna mouths as the security staff spring to their feet.

I decide to look down at my feet. Eye contact is best avoided minutes before a game. I don't want a stranger, an acquaintance or a fan running up to me with offerings of bravado or luck. As my steps quicken to reach the entrance,

Aruna looks hazy in the distance. My opponent, Vladimir Kramnik, assumes form ahead of me. The arbiter wears a polite smile as we take our seats. I adjust my knights to face the enemy forces. It's a quirk I carry.

Kramnik is hunched over the board, his elbows resting on the table. We've known each other since our teens, but for this match we're nothing other than exacting rivals. Only one of us will go home a World Champion.

Kramnik pushes his queen's pawn to the centre, with 1.d4.

Que sera sera, I tell myself, as I sip my tea. I mirror his move and nudge my Black queen's pawn by two squares.

ONE

DITCHING THE LADDER

OF GUT, HEART AND A WINNING IDEA

I SANK INTO THE FLUFFY BED OF THE HOTEL ROOM IN MEXICO city, feeling like a World Champion. Typically, a win keeps me awake, but tonight I'd given up even the pretence of sleep.

It was 30 September 2007, and a few hours since I'd been titled the undisputed World Champion. It was the kind of win that was supposed to get people to shut up; yet I wondered why I wasn't feeling more unbridled, slightly pompous or a little chaotic in my joy.

I was still stuffed from the Mexican dinner of gambas al pil pil, a Basque dish of shrimps in garlic and chilli oil, with chipotle and guacamole. The organizers of the World Championship tournament, Jorge and Veronica Saggiante, had treated my team and me to a celebratory meal at a fine Mexican restaurant housed in a stately mansion. Aruna, my trainer Nielsen, and my friend Hans-Walter Schmitt were all there – a small, tight group that was pretty much family. I'd cut into a chocolate cake that read '*Felicidades*', congratulations, in white frosting as the traditional Mexican musical ensemble of Mariachis played outside.

At 37, it was my second World Championship win, I had previously won in Tehran in 2000, but this felt new and validatory. The chess community had been dismissive of my Tehran accomplishment (the theme was essentially, 'Yes, you're World Champion, but...') and an annoying feeling had tailed me since. I wasn't entirely certain whether they adopted this stance to get me ruffled or they genuinely believed I was undeserving of the distinction. It was almost as if my Tehran World Championship title had been graded, labelled and ranked – and I stood at the bottom of the class. It's like feeling the tape snap across your chest at the finish line and then being told you still have a few more laps to go.

The split in the chess world lay at the heart of the questions over my status as the World Champion. Since the time that the former champion Garry Kasparov and his challenger to the title, Nigel Short, had broken away from the world governing body of the sport, Fédération Internationale des Échecs, FIDE, in 1993, world chess hadn't been the same. The two players staged their World Championship match under the aegis of a new body they had cobbled together, the Professional Chess Association (PCA), which would eventually run dry of funds and shut shop after my 1995 match against Kasparov. The standoff, though, continued.

I didn't feel compelled to pick a side. Those in either clique, I felt, were in it for themselves, and I didn't want to be the shmuck buying into their story. I was an aberration in an ecosystem where the top players were either Russian-backed, like Kramnik, or buffered and bankrolled by the powers that were, like Bulgaria's Veselin Topalov. It was only prudent then that I looked out for myself. My rationale for staying out of chess politics was simple: The ones whose side you are on conclude you chose them because you think they are the messiah bringing you to deliverance, while everyone in the rival group hates you passionately – and, unlike many of the others, I didn't really have an establishment backing me. Of course, I caught some flak for 'playing it safe'. Personally, though, it was a good decision. I'm not the kind of person who can play well while simultaneously waging three battles off the board. My chess would have flagged had politicking taken up my mind space, and I was very aware that once my performance dropped I would simply become irrelevant to the whole discourse. It made sense to just stick to what I did best: Shut the world out and play chess.

In the beginning, the split came across as a good thing. We had two sets of everything – competitions and champions, primarily. Till 1995, it even seemed to be progressing fairly systematically. But once the PCA disappeared, there was a definite slump in the organization of matches. Slowly, we realized that the two feuding organizations had only tainted the whole sport and turned the chess world into a murky place.

Meanwhile, Kasparov's search for an opponent and a sponsor continued, and he suggested I play him in a match in June 1999. The proposed match fell through a few months later since no sponsor came on board. In March the following year, the proposition resurfaced. This time I was circumspect, and since its organization and sponsorship details were largely sketchy, I chose to decline. The opportunity then passed on to Kramnik, who agreed to play Kasparov, and in November 2000, a month before I became the FIDE World Champion in Tehran, he beat Kasparov to become the Classical World Champion in a match sponsored by Brain Games.

Soon after Tehran, at a subliminal level, I struggled to prove my worth as champion. There was no big match on the horizon at which I could do so. It was frustrating since the schism in the chess world and its attendant problems weren't really my fault. Even winning the World Rapid Championship in 2003 through a two-game knockout final against Kramnik had done little to change my story. The 'but' that had continued to follow the reference to me as World Champion then switched to 'Ah, well, it's only rapid chess.'

Kasparov retired in 2005, while still at No. 1, and, in its efforts to unify the chess world, FIDE turned to the man who'd beaten him: Kramnik. The world body staged an ill-tempered match between its cycle champion, Topalov, and Kramnik in 2006, which the latter went on to win. Kramnik now had FIDE on a leash. He demanded that whoever won the eight-player, double round robin 2007 World Championship tournament in Mexico would play him in a match (best of 12 games) the following year.

Kramnik's team was antsy right through the Mexico tournament. They attempted to rush me into an agreement for the World Championship lined up for 2008. I was caught in a seemingly lost rook endgame against Alexander Grischuk in the thirteenth and penultimate round when Kramnik's manager, Carsten Hensel, reached out to Aruna, requesting a meeting with her to discuss and pencil in the contractual terms for a match that was still a year away. I was the sole leader with 8 points up to the penultimate round, certain to win the title, with Boris Gelfand behind me at 7 points, and their offer was one that was dismissive of my impending World Champion status. It was almost as if they were suggesting that I could rightfully stake claim to being a champion of any worth only if I beat Kramnik.

Aruna handled the negotiations by herself, stood her ground and refused to be hustled into any sort of immediate agreement. She even suggested they arrange a match with Gelfand instead, if they were in such a hurry. It was already a rottenly unfair deal. I'd won FIDE World Championship titles in both the knockout and tournament formats in Tehran and Mexico respectively, but still had to offer proof of my worth in a match against a player who had finished behind me in a World Championship tournament. More bizarrely, Kramnik's team proposed that I should 'under no circumstances' speak in German during the entire duration of the championship. I owned a house in the German town of Bad Soden, was a regular at the chess Bundesliga and made a clutch of appearances on local television channels there, so my ability to hold a conversation in the language was fairly above average. Kramnik spoke only Russian and English, so I could see why my communicating in the language of the local press would upset him. Of course, we found no logic in acceding to their request. There was a certain firmness we had to employ to mark our territory and to convey that they couldn't talk away my World Champion status.

It wasn't just the Russian player's squad giving us a hard time. At the press conference that followed my win in

Mexico, a journalist, who appeared to have been deputed to accentuate my doubts, asked me if I was ready for the match in Bonn. It was almost like the title I'd won minutes ago meant nothing. Though I had a good mind to wave him aside, I gritted my teeth and managed a fairly civil response.

Later that night, as I sat at the table in our hotel suite, mildly relieved that I wouldn't have to wake up to a high-pitched alarm and a game the next day, I was smacked by the thought that in exactly 12 months I would have to play Kramnik. It wasn't a particularly comforting idea. In over 50 classical games, from our first duel in 1989 up until Mexico, I had stacked up four wins and six losses against him. The remaining 40 games were drawn. If I lost in Bonn, the title of World Champion would slip away from me and it would soon be forgotten that I had ever earned it. There are players you hate losing to. For me, Kramnik was one of them. I'd flog myself mentally whenever I lost to him.

Our playing styles were in wild contrast. I was primarily a 1.e4 player, while he was known to be a 1.d4 exponent. Both are initial White pawn moves. The king's pawn opening, or 1.e4, is usually chosen by dynamic players looking for initiative early in the game, as opposed to the positional player's delight of 1.d4, or the queen's pawn opening, preferred by those who thrive on long, strategic warfare. My idea was to pursue sharp lines, where every move can tip the balance, and hunt for novelties. To labour and amble my way through 1.e4 also heightened the possibility of not finding open variations and running into the roadblocks that Kasparov had found himself confronted with during his match against Kramnik in 2000. With 1.d4, I would also be averting his favourite drawing weapons for 1.e4 – the Petroff Defence, a symmetrical opening for Black, which can be tough to crack, and the Berlin Variation of the Spanish opening, a solid yet underestimated opening for Black that had gone into cold storage until Kramnik had revived it with a host of new ideas, one of his greatest creative achievements, to hold Kasparov to four draws during their World Championship match.

I wasn't as dogmatic about 1.e4 as the former great Bobby Fischer was quoted as saying about his own stance on that position and I had dabbled in the queen's pawn opening in my earlier games. Though such efforts were largely pooled in rapid and blitz, I had employed the opening roughly 85 times from the White side.

The king's pawn opening, though, was closely entwined with my insignia as a player. It's also the square I autographed when fans at tournaments laid out their chessboards before me. It's where my opponents would hope to find me. I had no doubt that Kramnik too was likely to anticipate the same.

I wondered if I wanted to thrash around with preparations in an opening I'd wrung dry with use. It would be an effort, like squeezing water out of a rock. I could feel a buzz of energy at the mere thought of veering off the usual path. Almost like an epiphany, it struck me that I could in fact play Kramnik's own pet opening, the 1.d4, against him. It was a gut feeling, an impulse, accompanied by no pangs of guilt. I was eager to try something different and felt ready to face the risks that playing the move would entail. In my excitement, I would say I was almost flippant about the consequences.

My train of unspoken thoughts was interrupted when the door swung open and Nielsen walked in. Nielsen and I had first met when we played each other in the second round of the 2001 World Championship, which I won with Black. I noticed then that he had a sound opening preparation. He seemed remarkably warm, friendly and unaffected for someone who had just lost a game. We got talking and when, in 2005, I sought his assistance for the World Championship in San Luis, he readily agreed. He had stuck by my side since, uncomplaining of endless travels for tournaments and relishing the curd rice and paneer butter masala that Aruna cooked for him at home. He was my sounding board, the guy who posed unending questions till I concluded that a plan was flawed or became convinced of its perfection.

'Why don't I open with the 1.d4 against Kramnik?' I said, in a half-soliloquy, half-statement directed to my tiny audience. Aruna and Nielsen exchanged glances and waited in silence for me to provide a rationale. I didn't offer one right away. Even if my declaration had surprised him, Neilsen, his large frame now leaning over the table, didn't shoot down the idea or dismiss it summarily. He suggested we methodically run a check of its pros and cons. Seated at the foot of the bed, Aruna probably thought I was blabbering in my sleep-deprived state, an excess a chess player may be allowed after a fortnight of continuous play. She was perhaps certain that the radical idea would be forgotten at the breakfast table the next morning.

But that was not how it turned out.

As I stood on the podium at the closing ceremony of the

Mexico championship the following day, a bright-pink serape draped over my right shoulder, a gold medal and laurel wreath suspended around my neck, aware of Kramnik in attendance in the audience, I told myself I had to cling to my impulse, climb up the imaginary ladder, then push it away and continue climbing without its support. This technique is an excellent antidote to indecision and the only way you can make sure that you keep moving forward. It's what I often do when faced with challenging scenarios or when I yearn to switch back from a difficult but beneficial plan to a fairly simple though unreasonable one – I keep putting off taking a decision till it's too late and I'm so far down the path that going back is no longer an option.

No matter what I did, I knew I'd go into the match with Kramnik as the slightly ill-equipped player because, well, I was entering the combat zone using my opponent's weapon of choice. While there was sufficient time for me to wade into the preparations for the surprise plan, it was in no way enough to catch up on a lifetime's worth of experience playing it. After all, this was not an opening that I was thoroughly familiar with and I could play blind. A certain amount of evolution is built into chess as a sport – it requires you to constantly keep up with new moves and lines of play because each new game played is published and converted into common knowledge. To remain in competitive mode, it then becomes imperative to learn new pathways and append them to the existing cluster. Yet, players often linger in their favourite openings and counters, which is also fair since they might prefer to stick to known paths because they are perhaps good at them or have positive memories associated with them.

It wasn't so much the study of an underused opening that was my concern here as all the little angles to playing it that hadn't been explored, the many answers I didn't know that existed, or its various consequences. If the plan went awry, I would come across as pea-brained and half-witted.

As a long-term strategy, though, predictability is clearly among the worst. And, in all of this, your attitude should trump the decision itself. I assumed full responsibility for the decision, right from the time it occurred to me, and resolved to live with the fallout, good or ugly. I decided not to let the thought of possible negative outcomes bother me. The way I saw it, if I was thrown into an unfamiliar position, there was a good chance I would be able to improvise since I'd be free of the burden of precedents set by previous games I'd played. The primary allure for me was to be able to approach the match with a measure of excitement and the thrill of having taken a risk. I found it massively liberating. Sometimes it's wonderful to want to do things for the art, for the sport, rather than overthink and plan it down to the last detail. In general, it's also harder to be forgetful in areas that are fresh, new and rousing than those that are staid and everyday. Even if I were to be stuck, at least I'd be stuck in new, boring positions instead of old, boring ones. Deep within, I knew if I didn't bring myself to stick by this decision and wound up my career without taking risks, I'd hate myself – and I'd hate chess.

As the felicitations wound to a close in Mexico, my mind raced to the white kitchen in our home in Collado Mediano, a small, tranquil town 50 kilometres away from Madrid. Sometime in mid-2006, our friend Frederic Friedel, who co-founded and ran ChessBase, a firm that dealt in chess software and news, called to brief me about Kramnik dictating the terms for the Bonn match. I'd just towelled off after a workout at home and was irked by the discriminatory nature of the agreement. I joined Aruna in the kitchen and relayed the news to her. We both agreed that it was downright unjust that one player got to strut around with his privileges on display in such a brazen fashion. My sympathies then had been in earnest with whoever ended up winning in Mexico and had to play another match in a year's time to be counted as a fitting champion. 'Imagine the plight of that guy,' I had said then. 'The good thing is I don't need to worry about it right now. It's not my problem till it's my problem.'

Turns out I was that guy.

Viswanathan Anand v. Vladimir Kramnik (½–½)

(White)   (Black)

Game 2, 2008 World Championship, Bonn

DRAW

When I finally executed the queen's pawn opening, the surprise I'd kept under wraps, I did so with a hint of trepidation, wondering how the risk would pay off. I had decided to ditch the ladder and take the proverbial leap over a year ago, assumed responsibility for its consequences, and my team and I had worked very hard to make it happen. Now, I could finally play the kind of game I wanted.

♛

As a long-term strategy, being predictable is not of much advantage – for your career or business or even for yourself. Once in a while, you've got to take the counter-intuitive path, but not without owning responsibility for the consequences – and certainly not without preparation. In such situations, your attitude should trump the decision itself. When you focus on previously unconsidered solutions to reach your end goal, don't let your mind wallow in indecision or imagined negative outcomes. Instead, push through with execution.

TWO

STICKY NOTES

MADRAS, MANILA, MADRID AND EVERYTHING IN BETWEEN

WHEN I WAS YOUNG, I LOATHED TENNIS LESSONS.

Not because I minded the sport – it was the groggy early mornings at the academy in Egmore, Madras (now Chennai), and the endless rounds of jogging along the perimeter of the court that put me off. I was barely seven then and part of the junior programme at the academy run by noted Madras-based coach Robin Manfred less than 5 kilometres away from the Railway bungalows on Sterling Road, where we lived. The jogs were meant to serve as warm-ups for the lessons to follow, but I rarely got a chance to smack the ball. We were bunched into groups and got to play just four forehands and four backhands each – and it was a wrap. The next group would troop on to the court right after. It appeared to me to be too little a payoff for waking up at 5.30 a.m., and I wondered why my parents were paying good money to have me run around a court. It was a let-down after the lofty fantasies I had of myself chipping, charging and volleying like my hero, John McEnroe. My extreme admiration for the reviled, tantrum-throwing tennis star, who sported a halo of combed-out curls and a bright-red sweatband, was at odds with my quiet, unobtrusive nature. I didn't have his swagger or his fury. Thankfully, I had chess.

My mother belonged to a family of lawyers who played chess at home and she picked up the sport early. Much like the youngest child in almost any household, I was eager to participate in all the activities that my older siblings engaged in. She had introduced chess to my brother, older than me by thirteen years, and my sister, eleven years my senior – and I moved my first piece when I was six. My mother was as good at the game as one could get playing at home without formal training and was soon getting beaten by me at the board. One day, my sister happened to spot a signboard that read 'Chess Club' outside a building on her way back home from college and told us excitedly about it. On investigating, it turned out to be the Mikhail Tal Chess Club, named after the former Soviet great, housed at the Soviet Cultural Centre in the leafy, upscale, central Madras neighbourhood of Alwarpet.

India didn't have a Grandmaster (GM) yet and Manuel Aaron, who was the only International Master (IM) in the country when I started out, was one of the founding members of the Tal Chess Club. He was a dedicated champion of the game and had learnt Russian so he could read chess books in the language. That the club was established and thrived was no accident since the Cold War was raging then, and the Soviets were looking for a means to further their propaganda and footprint. The club even received free chess sets and books. The year the Tal Chess Club was set up, 1972, was also when the city of Reykjavik on the coast of Iceland played host to a match between Bobby Fischer and Boris Spassky, further fanning the already soaring geopolitical tensions between the Western and Eastern blocs. I was three when that match was played, so even though I grew up reading about its tempestuous nature and political overtones, it didn't leave the sort of indelible impression on me like it did on the previous generation.

Soon, I was hanging around at the Tal Club, awkward, fidgety and sheepish, watching older people play. I was too shy to propose to start a game, and wasn't sure if I should simply occupy a place at a table or wait to ask someone if I could. An affable gentleman named Keshavan, who ran the everyday affairs of the club, goaded me to join in the games and my mother asked him to have my name included in all the weekend tournaments the club hosted. Three days after joining the club, I played my first tournament. I wasn't sure if it was a bright idea, but when you're young, optimism is hardly a problem. I lost my first three games quite promptly, and anxiously counted down the clock when my fourth opponent didn't show up on time. Thankfully, he didn't turn up at all and my first win in chess was in fact by default.

It was the pre-Internet era, so chess books were the sole gateway to information. The usual drill was to wait for a relative or acquaintance who lived abroad or visited foreign shores to get you a book you wanted. My sister once picked up a copy of *Chess Openings: Theory and Practice* by Israel Albert Horowitz for me from a local bookstore, which I devoured from cover to cover and swore by with complete and unshakeable faith. For me, everything that book said was the word of god, to be believed, followed and never questioned, and for many years after that my opening repertoire, the collection of openings I dipped into regularly, was drawn solely from the book. Later, I got hold of José Raúl Capablanca's *Chess Fundamentals*, *1000 Miniature Openings* and a few other books that dealt with how to avoid opening traps and swindles.

When I was a little over eight, my father was commissioned on a special assignment of the Indian Railways and we moved to Manila for a year and a half. My brother and my sister were already pursuing a career and higher studies respectively, so I was the only one who accompanied my parents to the Philippines. We landed there in November 1978, a month after the bizarre, bitter World Championship match between Anatoly Karpov and Viktor Korchnoi was held in Baguio City. It was a postcard-pretty hillside resort and my parents took me to the venue where the match had been played. For a boy of my age, it was hard to be greatly inspired by a hall full of empty chairs, no matter how vivid the descriptions were of a World Champion pacing its length. Once I'd seen the chairs, I was simply more interested in getting back to my comics. It only stirred into significance when I won my World Junior Championship title at the venue nine years later.

Finding myself in a country that was right in the midst of a chess boom was a godsend. Philippines was home to Asia's first Grandmaster, Eugenio Torre, and my mother persisted in not letting my affinity for the sport slacken. In fact, she took it several steps ahead. She began by rifling through the phonebook, looking up every single 'Torre' in the country until her search was narrowed down to the most likely Torre. When she called on the number she'd diligently circled, it turned out that while she'd found the right Torre household, she'd got hold of the wrong brother. Luckily, the brother was a chess coach and was kind enough to suggest a good chess club for me to frequent. I wound up not attending chess lessons in Manila, though I participated in the weekend tournaments at a nearby club. Our primary mode of commuting in Manila were the kitsch, vibrantly painted Jeepneys. They were essentially United States Army jeeps that had been abandoned by the troops after World War II. Formerly used for transporting soldiers, the Jeepneys could ferry 20 to 25 passengers each and was something of a Filipino ingenuity icon. My mother and I would take them to and from the club, and a good game meant that I would be treated to a bucket of ice cream with tiny chunks of jelly and nuts in it at the parlour right next to our house. It was what I looked forward to the most after a win.

In the beginning, a trainer was hired to help me with my game. He ran me through bishop endings and it soon became evident that I already knew most of what he was trying to teach me, so the sessions were called off. While I was away at school during the afternoons, my mother would watch a one-hour chess show on television called *Chess Today*, which analysed the games of leading players. At the end of each episode, the show's presenter would leave the viewers with a chess position to solve, answers to which had to be submitted via post. The winners were mailed a chess book as a prize. My mother would diligently note down every position explained during the show, sometimes even taping episodes for us to watch later, and once I was home from school we'd work on the puzzle together, solve it and post the answer. I began winning so frequently that the guys at the television station were at their wits' end. They asked me to visit their library and help myself to as many books as I wanted, on the condition that I wouldn't send in any more answers.

It was not just chess that my mother gave me company in. She learnt swimming too, so she could be with me in the pool at our home in Manila and offered herself up to be something of a lifeguard as I splashed around. She was indulgent in her affection towards me. Once, after I nagged her over the surprised looks my classmates exchanged upon seeing her pick me up from school in a saree, she bought herself Western clothes so she could wear them when she accompanied me.

♛

We returned to Madras in 1980, when I was eleven, and I rejoined my tennis classes. My days ran to a packed schedule: Wake up at 5 a.m., reach the tennis academy in half an hour, return home, shower, change, rush to school and, after classes were done, head over to the Tal Club. Pretty soon it was clear that my tennis was going nowhere but my chess was, so I dropped out of tennis and was happy to allow myself an extra hour of sleep in the morning.

That year, I had my first interaction with a Grandmaster when the Latvian–Soviet player Vladimir Bagirov visited

Chennai. I was among the roomful of schoolchildren against whom he played a simultaneous exhibition game. At one stage of the game, I offered him a draw. He looked at me, then at my board, picked up his rook and my bishop and, in a thick Russian accent, asked me why I had made him the offer. It was my first lesson in piece evaluation and his spurning my offer made me realize that you don't always get a draw when you offer one.

I was by then a pro at the customary five-minute blitz games that were played at the club. By way of rule, it allowed winners to keep their place at the table, while the ones who lost had to get back in the queue and wait for another turn. Often, it would be me sitting tight at one end of the table with my opponents at the other end changing with every game. Unlike the tennis classes, here I got to play as much as I wanted. Competitions organized by age group were rare then, and you had to hold your own against players of all strengths and sorts. Frequent matches also meant that I was exposed to fresh theories and varied styles of play, and this experience not only effectively cut down on learning time but also added exponentially to my growth as a player. At the club, however, I was looked upon as the cocky boy who would beat the older players at blitz and interrupt the lectures conducted by Manuel Aaron on the tactics used by Soviet Grandmasters with unsolicited suggestions on alternate moves. A fellow player once complained to my mother that I was badly behaved. It came as a surprise to me since that was hardly my nature or my intention.

I put myself through a manic number of local tournaments in 1981. It was also the year I played chess with my mother for the last time. We had gone to Shimla on a family holiday and one evening, thanks to a terrible hailstorm, we found ourselves stuck in our hotel room. With nothing else to do, we played Monopoly, my favourite board game then, next to chess, but soon my mother and I were launching our bishops and knights at each other. I came up with a highly ridiculous opening scheme and, even though I was a much stronger player than her, I lost. We never sat across a board to play each other after that, though we did continue to discuss chess and she travelled with me for tournaments.

I began to get noticed on the national scene after I won the title of National Sub-junior Chess Champion in 1983. My mother's cousin, who lived in Goa, played host to us when we travelled there for the tournament and a standout memory I have of the trip is of the food she served us, particularly a scrumptious vegetable au gratin that she'd mastered from the popular Indian author Tarla Dalal's recipe books. Other aspects of the tournament turned out to be just as enjoyable, particularly my wins.

That year I also defeated the nine-time national champion and my former tutor at the Tal Chess Club, Aaron, at the National Team Championship in Bombay. I was thirteen then. It was the second time in two years that I'd pulled off a win against him. The previous instance was at the 1982 District Team Championship in Chennai. The Indian Institute of Technology (IIT) Bombay campus, in Powai, played host to the national championship and though the Madras district chess association had taken the ambitious decision to field a team of promising teens from the state, the Madras Colts, they had no money to fund our participation. Consequently, renowned Indian playback singer S.P. Balasubrahmanyam stepped in and agreed to sponsor the team. For some reason, I was under the impression that I should offer up to Mr Balasubrahmanyam, as a sign of gratitude for his benevolence, the little money my mother had entrusted me with. Thankfully, better sense prevailed, and I didn't go through with it. During my game against Aaron, I was miserably sick, shaking with fever, and I turned up at the board swathed in woollens in the sultry heat of May. I ended up beating him and won the top board prize. The Aaron game was for me the starting point of a long, unbroken streak of success. It was the payoff for the work I'd put in until then – though I was quite oblivious of this at the time. The following year, I earned an IM title and before my sixteenth birthday I became the national champion.

♛

Our earliest lessons are seared into our minds and hearts. A habit I grudgingly picked up as a child on my mother's insistence was writing down my impressions immediately after a game; typically, a loss. When you're young, you don't find any pressing need to live up to a routine, and back then I did it more for my mother's satisfaction than for my benefit. I'd methodically write the notations down in neat letters and often underline – with a belligerent double streak – the notes on the portions of the game where I'd blundered. As I grew older, this practice slowly grew on me. Putting down my observations right after a defeat when the pain was raw and the sting was fresh, I stumbled upon the solutions I had seen but didn't act upon or the ones I had overlooked. Not only did it help me spot my mistakes but it also gave me a macro perspective of whether the misses fit into some sort of a worrying pattern that needed to be eliminated. After a win, I'd usually allow myself some room and stay away from this process a little longer before the cadaver was laid out for close examination. I was still curious to know if I played a line in the best way possible, but the urge was not as strong as it was following defeats or missed opportunities. It was also a brilliant way to funnel my emotions after a game – angst, remorse or delirium – and study the results objectively. Once this practice became routine, after every game I couldn't wait to revisit what I did or didn't do. Suddenly, I began to feel that without that understanding my experience was almost incomplete.

Over time, I began widening the scope of my notes – jotting down my opponents' quirks, propensities, gestures and all the little things that tended to distract me before or during a game. To caution myself against blitzing when I'm tense during a game, my note reads: 'When you're almost winning and have more time than your opponent, DO NOT make a move. Pull your hand back. Get up, drink tea, wash your face, take a deep breath and then come back to the board.' For rapid tie-breaks, I remind myself to roll up my sleeves so they don't hinder the speed of my movements on the board. I even have notes nudging myself to be more attentive to certain particulars while playing against specific opponents. Levon Aronian, for one, has a habit of striking up conversation on the morning of a game if he's feeling upbeat. It could just be playful banter about how he's going to give me a hard time. My self-admonishing note for this kind of a situation says: 'Don't get into any small talk. Stop making jokes and pretending to be funny.'

Often, I'm amazed when I dig up old notations, and think, 'Wow, it seems to me now that I did everything beautifully... But at that moment, I was struggling, stuttering, hesitating and just generally hating myself.' At times, after games, I've been tired and put off the self-chastising exercise for later. But by the next morning the intensity is gone. What ends up as notes then is a paraphrase of a paraphrase. It's a hit-and-miss scenario, because the immediacy is lost. All that the brief notes that I scribble with half a heart after a late breakfast the morning after a game tell me now is that I survived. So, really, the fresher the notes, the more useful they are. My notes have served me well over the years and have transformed into a manual of sorts, reminding me of the pitfalls and the advantages I may come across. I go back to them often, particularly if I'm returning to playing tournaments after a self-imposed break. The practice may have taken a slight punch over the years and I may not be as methodical as I used to be about them, but at 50, it's a habit I still keep up, even if in its abridged version.

♛

As a young player, the one title I fervently chased for two years was that of Grandmaster. India didn't have a

Grandmaster then and my pursuits revolved around that one giant dream. At the Tata Steel Grandmaster Tournament in Calcutta in 1986, I missed my first Grandmaster norm by half a point, and at the Lloyds Bank Masters Open held later that year in London, it eluded me again by half a point. I was promoted to the top board and scored 7.5 points out of a possible 11 at the Chess Olympiad that year in Dubai, but a norm continued to be out of reach. Though there was no risk of failure involved in the pursuit, since no one had done it before in the country, I still felt frustrated over missing it by the narrowest of margins.

Arbiter Stewart Reuben had in an earlier conversation in London told me that it was possible that I would keep missing the norms for months and then suddenly turn into a Grandmaster almost effortlessly. I had listened to him sceptically then, but that's exactly how it happened.

The World Junior Chess Championship title in 1987 finally gave me a norm, and subsequently in New Delhi, I picked up the second norm with a draw in the final round. My mother kept me away from distractions so that I wouldn't slip into my usual tendency to relax early when things were going my way and losing a game. I finally won the title of Grandmaster with the third and final norm, after a draw in the penultimate round at the Shakti Finance International Chess Tournament in Coimbatore in 1988. To this day, I recall Reuben's advice, and I find it to be relevant still. It always makes sense to keep working at goals without obsessing over how far you're from it or how hopelessly you're missing the mark each time. If you persevere, it will eventually be yours.

In hindsight, I realize I was incredibly lucky throughout this time. Teenagers in sports careers have academics to juggle, and their hesitation to invest time and effort entirely into sport stems from the obvious fear of falling behind their peers in studies. Here, the risk–reward ratio comes into play. In my case, the breaks I needed to get ahead in my chess career came at opportune moments – I became national champion in the tenth standard, and Grandmaster two years later, when I was leaving school and getting ready for college. I was ranked fifth in the world when I finished my bachelor's degree in commerce. Essentially, the rewards kept trickling in at the stages of my life when I would have had to weigh my options. The protracted process of deciding between a dedicated sporting career and higher studies, which my peers obsessed over, was alien to me.

It is easy to lose perspective if you head into a career dedicated to a sport at too young an age. It could make relating to different people, situations and even everyday living quite challenging. It's best to find a hobby or a pursuit removed from your sport – for me it was astronomy, studying the sciences and maths. It's a lot like our school holidays as I remember them. The day after school heads into a summer break, you're madcap-crazy with joy, but if you don't engage your brain in some way soon enough, it begins to feel more like drudgery and less like a holiday. After two weeks of your holiday, when you still have six weeks left, every day feels like every other day and time just drags. If you have hobbies to pursue, the days seem to disappear. Similarly, in chess, it's much easier to take your mind off a painful defeat or a run of poor form if you find joy and interest in other avenues. It's difficult if chess is all you know. For the brilliant and gifted Fischer, this had proved to be true. He was unable to detach himself from the sport. We've all learnt as many lessons from his life as from his games – both inspiring and cautionary. His chess is hard not to admire, and he made it possible for players after him to be professionals and make a living from playing chess. In many ways, we're standing on the shoulders of greats such as him.

If juxtaposed, I consider my journey in the sport to be much easier than someone like Fischer's. In his time, he really had to give up everything to become a chess player. I didn't. Our environment plays a huge role in how our brain is stimulated, the interests we develop, and how we view and nurture them. The early impression you have of a subject and the climate in which you acquire the impression can have a big impact on you. I wasn't browbeaten into picking up chess or playing it. My parents left it to me to divide my time between my studies and chess. Their attitude freed up my mind and put me at ease, and enabled me to fall back on either, as it suited me. Chess for me had no pangs or pressure tied to it.

The time after I won the title of Grandmaster brought with it my first experience of the aftermath of obsessively chasing a goal. I was suddenly left without a purpose. I felt empty and bored, almost listless. All this while, I had been solely fixated on a singular pursuit. But once I got to my destination I kept looking back rather than at fresh peaks. I didn't know what to do with myself. Tournaments and scores didn't excite me any more, and my results took a beating.

For six months I was caught on a conveyor belt of despair. It was through my interactions with other Grandmasters on my travels for overseas tournaments that I realized this was a normal phase and one that almost all players experienced. Sometimes, a goal can be such a big deal, such an all-consuming theme in our lives, that we just don't know what to look forward to any more after we've achieved it. Gradually, I managed to pull myself back together, just in time for the next phase of my life as a chess player to begin.

Before 1991, I travelled to and from Europe playing tournaments while often toying with the idea of finding a base there. It seemed like a sensible way to cut down on the constant travel and its attendant expenses, and could open up doors for regular participation in the tournaments held around the continent. Proximity meant visibility, which in turn led to organizers constantly having me at the back of their minds. When I lived in India, they presumed that since flights were long and few, I would not make it anyway. Once I moved to Europe, this changed. Organizers began calling me to check on my availability if another player withdrew from a tournament. A close friend, Albert Toby, lived in Amsterdam, and it seemed like a fairly good choice of a city to live in. We looked at a few options but somehow the details didn't fall into place.

Amsterdam fell off my plans once I ran into a fresh set of parents at the Linares International Chess Tournament in February 1991.

Mauricio Perea, or Maurice, and his wife, Nieves, were an elderly couple who'd retired to a life of following chess and football, and helped put together the event in Linares, then a small mining town in Andalusia.

In the round robin tournament, Maurice watched in bewilderment as I took up little time on my clock, my hands whirring over the board as I made my moves at blinding speed against Jaan Ehlvest in round 4. He came over to check if my clock was working at all, since it had barely eaten up any time. The game ended in a draw and he invited me over for dinner that evening. As I chomped on the food, Maurice, his voice full of concern, advised me to think longer and play slower in the games ahead. With a hint of grin, I replied, 'Okay, Maurice, how about I take a minute more next time?' He broke into laughter and hugged me. Nieves fished a promise out of me that I'd take her out to the best Chinese restaurant in town if I beat one of the top guys (which isn't saying much, since Chinese joints in Linares were then only marginally better than the burger takeaways there).

Maurice and Nieves threw open their home in Collado Mediano to me, and Nieves spoilt me with her care – washing my clothes, sewing my buttons, cooking food and just stopping short of tucking me into bed. Maurice remained perplexed both by my sense of fashion and my choice of music. I would typically have on a pair of large white sneakers, my hands stuffed in the pockets of my baggy jeans, and be listening to the Irish rock band The Cranberries or the British synth-pop duo of the Pet Shop Boys on my Walkman. For Maurice, an Englishman by birth and etiquette and a passionate devotee of Beethoven and Brahms, both my clothes and the music peddled by the bands whose beats I headbanged to were sacrilege and beyond comprehension. His favourite refrain was *'Caramba que ese so!* What is this noise?', alluding to my music, and he never stopped wondering aloud about my insistence on drizzling ketchup over my pasta.

But for all the things we did differently, we were united by a love for history, astronomy and, of course, chess. One of my abiding memories is of us lounging in patio chairs on the deck of their beautiful, sprawling five-bedroom home, taking in the scent of ferns, Arizona cypress and the earth, and watching the sun disappear behind the mountains in the horizon.

It was Maurice who bought me my first fine jacket – a checkered grey single-breasted piece from the Alta Moda boutique in Linares. Typically warm, affectionate and father-like, Maurice said, 'Vishy, you're not just a chess player any more. You're a future World Champion. You should now start dressing like one.'

Manuel Aaron v. Viswanathan Anand (0–1)
(White) (Black)

1982 District Team Championship, Madras
BLACK WINS

I vividly remember move 29 of this game, the Nxd4. White had masked its pieces – the king, queen, knights, everything on the kingside – and there was a rook on the third rank waiting to join the attack. At first, it looked hopeless. But then, Black brought in one more piece. It felt like reinforcements arriving in a battle. An army that was cornered suddenly found help.

♛

When I played this game with Manuel Aaron, my obsession with winning the Grandmaster title was still some years away. At the same time, my win was a culmination of everything I had learnt and worked for until then, with little else weighing on my mind. There's something to be said about working towards achieving a goal without obsessing over how far you're from it or how hopelessly you're missing the mark each time. Once you shut out the clamour of the result and simply persevere, success is bound to be yours.

THREE

THE ART OF REMEMBERING

HOOKS, HACKS AND SERENDIPITY

WHAT'S THE LAST THING THAT SLIPPED YOUR MIND? WAS IT a chore, your belongings at a hotel or on a flight, an appointment or, worse still, your wedding anniversary? If it's the last, I hope your limbs are intact.

I'm a survivor myself. I run the risk of throwing my reputation off the cerebral pedestal with this story, which I've often shared at seminars and gatherings – but I'll do it once more anyway. It was January 1998, during my World Championship match against Karpov in Lausanne, when three-and-a-half-inch floppy disks were still in vogue. Every night, whatever preparation had been worked on would be backed up, stored in floppies and stowed away in a safe by Aruna. One night, after putting away the disks, she turned to me with a knowing smile and told me that the code to unlock the safe was easy to recall, 2706. Confused, I commented, 'That's a silly code... Which player has a rating like that?' Live Elo ratings weren't around then and ratings were usually updated to a difference of five. Aruna looked aghast. From the look in her eyes I could sense her blood beginning to simmer. 'It's not anyone's rating,' she said coldly. 'It's our wedding anniversary!' I had the stupidest look on my face as I tried to make sense of why I should be trusted to remember this detail. We were just into the second year of our marriage.

Coming from a chess player who is believed to thrive on plucking out endless moves, games and notations from memory, this might sound incredulous, even blasphemous. Most of us players can recall moves from all the games we've played and yet it is also true that we can be at sea when it comes to a five-point grocery list. The pre-Internet, pre-mobile era now appears to be buried in a glacial past from a Pleistocene Age. Then, it was our spouses to whom we'd turn for reminders on everything (though maybe not the wedding anniversary!). Today, we're a bunch of hunched figures with our thumbs on rollers, flitting between mobile applications and tools, gyroscopes and location data. Google reminds me there's a flight to catch, pops up directions to a restaurant I'm about to visit, and on many days I have a birthday alarm going off, making me choke on my morning cereal, and I can't for the life of me remember whom I'd set it for.

Broadly, chess players tend to be the subject of envy for their eidetic memory – or at least what's commonly perceived as eidetic memory. This belief was debunked by the Dutch psychologist and chess player Adriaan de Groot more than half a decade ago through his experiments. He tested four categories of players of varying strengths – Grandmaster,

Master, expert and class 'A' player, the last a decent chess player who ranks below expert level. De Groot showed each of them a chessboard configuration with 22 pieces from an unknown game. The subjects were then asked to reconstruct the board, either on another board or verbally. The Grandmasters and Masters reproduced it almost effortlessly and got 93 per cent right, while the experts and class 'A' players struggled a bit, missing a detail in a couple of places, and got 72 per cent and 51 per cent correct respectively. But when the positions were randomized, making no logical sense whatsoever, each group, including the Grandmasters, placed only three or four pieces correctly. It showed that Grandmasters didn't look at or commit to memory the positions of individual pieces; rather, they remembered pieces in groups, structures or patterns.

So, essentially what chess players have isn't an inexplicably photographic memory, but contextual memory. What most of us do is convert a picture into a story. The mental soliloquy in a seasoned player's head goes something like this: 'Oh, these three pawns haven't been moved, so White was basically moving these other pawns… White has a bishop here, and I recall this bishop position from my game last year. Ah, this is a Nimzo-Indian opening [a hypermodern opening that doesn't involve fianchettoing a bishop at the start], so I know what the pawn structure should look like and all I have to remember is that one pawn is out of place on both sides – maybe a3 and a6, or a2 and a6 – and everything else slots in.' The reason the Grandmasters and Masters were able to reconstruct what they were shown the first time was because the picture made sense to them.

An equivalent of this would be showing the photograph of a landscape to an artist. It may have a few striking features, like a red boat with a name painted across it in white letters, a chapel on the bank of a river, and mountains and trees forming the backdrop. Like the Grandmasters, the artists will recall the features of the photo perfectly, but if they are shown a version of it in which the details are messed up – the boat is broken, the chapel is missing and 20 new objects are now visible in the background – they will have trouble recreating the original. Much like the Grandmasters, what these artists would do is take in a couple of crucial elements and fill in the rest of the background in their minds.

Personally, I favour creating summaries, or collapsing a whole lot of positions into a story. While doing this, I keep the essential elements in mind. I could liken this to a situation in which you've lost your way and all you know is that you need to head north-west. With that basic information, even without the exact address of your destination or a set of directions, you might still find your way there. It works in the same way as a person recalling trivia through a story that makes the facts stick in their head. Who's ever going to forget Isaac Newton and the discovery of gravity, for example? An apple falling on his head while he was sitting in the garden and the flash of brilliant insight that inspired the understanding of gravitational force is perhaps the best-known anecdote in the study of science. The story that goes with the discovery makes it unforgettable.

When I was younger, I could recall every game I played from the first move till the end. Now, with an avalanche of analysis and positions to remember, I often don't have complete memory of a game I played a week ago. Of course, I may have stored away in my mind key details like the opening and perhaps some critical mistakes, but if I'm asked to replay all 40 moves I may have made I will perhaps need to check my notes. Similarly, in my younger years, I could rattle off all the phone numbers I'd ever dialled, but now I don't look up a number any more, only the contact list on my phone. So that part of my memory lies unused and has become rusty.

At simultaneous matches – where one Grandmaster plays against a group of amateurs – I've often watched the jaws of teens with wispy proto-moustaches drop when I've caught them out for removing a piece from the board while I was gone. It's a classic example of pattern recognition at play. What I have in mind are some key snippets – I know the boards where I'm a piece down and the ones where I'm not. If I've waded into some trouble at one of the boards, I remember it intensely, since a part of my brain is constantly scouting for a solution even while I'm attending to the other boards. I can tell when a piece is missing, not because I carry all 20 games in my head or recall the earlier positions exactly, but because the harmony on the board is disturbed. It's awfully hard to change the position of a piece without upsetting the harmony of the board. If there is no pawn structure, the kind of structure you'd find in a painting for instance, and it's just loose pieces and a single piece is displaced by a square, I might not notice. But if it's taken off the board, I'll spot it right away. There have been times when a piece has been sneakily removed and I've charged my opponent with, 'Hey, put back my piece,' much to his horror.

If disturbing a piece doesn't really alter the evaluation, I might not care much for it. I would suspect something is amiss, but let it pass. Similarly, if my opponent removes a piece which could potentially backfire on him and improves my position at that point, I might let him have it.

Playing a move on the board, however, is more than just about remembering. It's also about remembering why the move is being made. If I know for certain that a particular move works at a specific position, I can play it with a whole other level of confidence; on the other hand, if all I have is a broad idea of where a move might work, which then calls for rechecking, I'd play it with a hint of hesitation. In situations where I'm not sure which move will work in my favour but am certain of three moves that will *not* be of help, I can work through elimination, narrow down the possibilities and then make a move that will be of the greatest advantage to me.

Constantly revising and refreshing an idea or a line also helps its memory sink in deep. When I play a few games to go over these details, I can spot which variation I need to run a check on, which in turn allows me to focus on particulars instead of an abstract to-do list. During my World Championship matches, for instance, there were several stages to revising and reinforcing my memory. At training camps two or three months ahead of the match, often an 'outsider', that is, someone who was not part of my team of seconds, would be invited to play with me so that my response to the surprise value of fresh moves or ways of thinking could be tested. Ahead of the World Championship matches in Mexico, Bonn and Sofia, in 2007, 2008 and

2010 respectively, Magnus Carlsen, then a teen, came over to spar with me.

On the morning of a game during the World Championship matches, after breakfast, my team of four trainers and I would spend a couple of hours debating the final choices and lines, and they would force me to go over my notes before breaking off to get back to work while I showered and took a nap. In the final 45-minute stretch before heading off to the venue, I would sit at the board in the training room while my seconds stood around me, forming a half-moon and, by turns, throw positions at me to solve. If I was unable to solve a position in the third or fourth attempt and they were all standing around me, perhaps secretly wondering how I ever became a World Champion, the embarrassment I felt was intense and scalding. It was almost as if my ego was shredded into bits with a butcher's cleaver. If a similar position popped up in a game, I would never be in doubt any more – the humiliation I'd experienced earlier would work as a branding iron. Sometimes, having your ego take a knock before a game is actually a good thing. You're then a lot sharper at the board.

The rule of thumb for remembering deeply is to look at a position once, then not look at it for a day, then go over it once again and skip it for three days, and then go back and look at it yet again. By the eighth time you've looked at it, your brain has already encoded the memory and every time you come back to it, it only gets reinforced. In recent years, what I often do is take photographs of all the positions I want to revise and keep them on my phone. When I'm on a flight, I flip through them. The idea is to expose my brain to what I want it to recall. This exercise, though, is unlikely to offer results if done over too short a span of time. By the third time the brain may have switched off. If done on an irregular schedule for one or two weeks, by the end of the second week the image of the positions on the board would have lodged itself in the mind. Although, even that may not be permanent. It's helpful to revise the position or idea a month later, repeat the same after three more months and by the end of the year it should have set up camp in your brain. The only guarantee to remembering is periodic revision. The intervals can be lengthened, but at the end of each break there should be a refresher course waiting.

Even the things we know inside out are worth refreshing. It's like travelling back in time and remembering almost everything associated with a childhood photo when it is shown to you. It brings back recollections of the occasion when it was taken, what the setting was and even the emotions felt at the time. In chess, a lot of the work involves going over positions, lines, variations and ideas we already know, so we're essentially repeating our notes to ourselves. Once I establish an emotional connect with a particular pattern, it makes it harder to forget. My memory of positions and lines is much stronger if the reason for remembering them is interesting – a game connected to a painful loss, perhaps, or if something is new and interesting. If, as an example, I've experienced a crushing rook ending and lost a game, the next time I walk into a rook ending I will probably feel my hair stand on end and a trickle of sweat run down my back, because the memory of that painful defeat suddenly comes alive. There are childhood lessons I still haven't forgotten, from perhaps losing a match because I was hasty against an opponent at a club championship and then watching him smirk. To this day, when my hand is rushing to make a move, I stop myself.

Against Judit Polgár at the 2012 London Chess Classic, I played the Najdorf Sicilian, a popular response for Black to the king's pawn opening that can be both highly aggressive and positionally sound, and on move nine she nudged her queen diagonally by two squares, resting it on the f3 square. I had been nothing but a Najdorf player all my life, but since I had hardly needed it since 2008 I had stopped revising it. I knew I had to play one of the two queen moves that popped up in my head, but couldn't remember which one. I took a chance, pushed my queen by one square along the dark diagonal at c7, and suddenly my heart skipped a beat. I had a feeling I'd played the wrong move. It was made worse when a fellow participant walking past stopped in his tracks, looked at the board closely and then walked away. The warning gongs went off loudly in my head. I was certain I had blundered and the person who had walked past was now laughing at me. This, despite it being an opening I was supposed to know like the back of my hand. It was as elementary as knowing the way out of my house. Once I'd calmed down, I saw that the position clarified itself and there was no real threat to me. Memory is never fully discarded, but the brain keeps refreshing what is relevant for today and pushes other things into the background. With revision, it takes a lot less effort to recall what is in the background; without it, the memory remains out of reach, like the Najdorf did for me.

The trickier predicament in chess is that since every game that is played goes into a database, opponents are always referencing well-known moves and lines to create slightly modified, new problems. They say history doesn't repeat itself, but it often rhymes. To beat this, you have to keep revising your notes, run a check on your approaches through modern chess engines or computer programs that analyse positions and try newer paths. Once in a while you may run into the same conclusions – a position that is good for Black, for instance – but by not approaching them through hackneyed methods your knowledge of it becomes more sophisticated. If I start working on a new problem in the morning, by the evening I may discover 20 ways to tackle it. These 20 approaches will remain fresh in my head for at least a week afterwards. If one of them happens to be similar to a different position I worked on two months ago, that appends itself to the fresh learning. In effect, it's learning an old lesson a new way. Anything on the board that offers you two or three approaches to remembering it improves your chances almost by nine squares.

However, if the attempt is to cram a multitude of positions and lines into your memory without knowing which one to remember with the greatest intensity, it can always catch you unawares. The one thing you didn't check could be the one thing that crops up on the board. If I haven't revised my notes, the chances of me forgetting my preparation runs high. It's why my team's chorus cry for me during a World Championship is 'Revise, revise, revise.' 'Paint it Black' and 'Viva La Vida' can wait.

I wouldn't really brag about my memory to do with things outside of chess. I'm quite terrible with faces. Before a school reunion, I usually go through Facebook for recent pictures of my former classmates so I don't embarrass myself. I'm also culpable for forgetting start timings of tournaments. At the 1995 Intel Rapid Chess Grand Prix tournament in Paris, in what was supposed to be my first game against Kasparov after our World Championship match that year, I jumbled up the start time. It didn't work in my favour that I had confused trois (3 p.m.) and treize (thirteen, 1300 hours). I should have simply clarified the time in English. I walked into the hall only in time to play the second game, and that too because I'd decided to get there early to settle in!

It's similar with pairings. I don't forget pairings if I know the pairing numbers and can even reel off the pairings of an entire tournament. Often, I'll go up to the arbiter and inquire what the time control of the tournament I'm playing is. It's not that I've forgotten. It could well be a blitz tournament, but since the current tendency is to bunch tournaments in a group, it can get tough to remember, especially when the last three played were under different time controls.

I tend to remember alpha-numeric airport boarding gates according to chess opening codes. With books I've read or movies I've recently watched, I might be able to lay a finger on the storyline and the main characters, but the title may escape me. Often, I've checked out of a hotel, but left a belonging behind on the table of my room and it's struck me only at the airport boarding gate. Most frequently, it's my mouse pad. Here, the problem is not that I don't remember I brought a mouse pad along, but that the mouse pad is something I see lying on the table every day and it just blends in with the furniture. That makes it difficult to stay memorable.

I've also been guilty of misplacing at least half a dozen gemstone rings that I wore on my mother's insistence and her faith in their good providence. Of course, it was only the jeweller who had a good run of luck as the precious stones kept growing in size and value each time I lost one. Tired of my repeated carelessness, she eventually gave up buying them.

♛

Hooks – or things that arrest our attention – are particularly beneficial in chess.

Neuroscientists Michael Gazzaniga and Roger W. Sperry's split-brain research is now legendary. They were the first to investigate hemispheric lateralization to determine the extent to which the left brain and the right brain are specialized for certain functions. In the 1950s and 1960s, they carried out experiments on cats, monkeys and humans to study the differences in functionalities between the two hemispheres and concluded that the left brain is more dominant in speech and languages, while the right is more suited to visual–motor skills. Establishing these theories with an absolute finality, though, has proved impossible. The perception of chess as a left-brained activity executed with cold reason and calculation is not one I entirely agree with since emotional hooks such as a searing embarrassment or loss can be hard to forget. When I'm playing someone I earnestly don't want to lose to or personally dislike, my brain is sprightly, I uncover new resources and also tend to defend much harder.

There's still an element of ambiguity in neuroscience over how our brain organizes material and puts it to use when required, or how memories are formed, but there is no question about the fact that the human brain makes amazing connections between different and diverse pieces of information. One path of study into which I've tried to branch out is learning to play openings that are not part of my repertoire. I began by studying the games of Kramnik and Gelfand in which they used openings that were not part of my regular preparation. The Leningrad Variation of the Grünfeld Defence, for one. I would pore over their games without really anticipating an immediate use of my learnings. But the result was unexpected. I found that I could use those moves to at least gain a head start in positions where I had a deep pawn, and had to play effectively to gain initiative.

Vassily Ivanchuk once spoke to me about an opening in the Catalan and showed me a pretty idea where Black attacks White's queen, and White simply ignores the attack and moves his bishop. Afterwards, Black is left to choose between two bad options – the marginally better one being to move the queen away so that White goes on to capture a rook and a bishop. But White's dominance is already so great by then that the position is no good for Black. The alternative is to maintain the material balance, or the value of the pieces, but the difference in the piece placement becomes overwhelming. A month or so after my conversation with Ivanchuk, I was playing Joel Benjamin at the 1989 Wijk aan Zee tournament and we got into a position in the

Sicilian Defence, which is as far away from the Catalan as one can imagine, except, miraculously, I found that the idea Ivanchuk had outlined for me worked. Instead of long-term compensation, here I collected material. White would have had two knights on c4 and b5 attacking the Black queen, which would then have to be sacrificed. It caught Benjamin off guard and turned the game in my favour.

It's a good idea to expose your mind to different kinds of subjects for the fun of it, because you can never tell when they'll find a way to the forefront of your thoughts and effect a breakthrough. In this, Apple founder Steve Jobs's life story is compelling. His calligraphy lessons under an ex-Trappist monk at Reed College in Portland, learning about serif and sans serif typefaces and the varying of space between different letter combinations, ended up making all the difference.

Jobs was essentially a student of computer science and none of this was assumed to have any practical application in his career. Weirdly and wonderfully, it did. Ten years later, when his company was putting together the first Macintosh computer, Jobs said 'it all came back' to him. His calligraphy lessons, he reflected, were the reason for the Mac being the first computer with beautiful typography. Had he dropped that single course in college, the Mac would never have multiple typefaces or proportionally spaced fonts. My first thought when I read about this was how serendipitous it had been for Jobs – there was no way a man could, so early in his life, discern that one day a firm he would set up would be famed more for the design aesthetics of its products than for its area of specialization.

Jobs had a flamethrower's mind and was wildly passionate about stepping into new ventures. In an address to Stanford graduates he spoke of how we can't connect the dots looking forward, but only join them looking backwards – we have to trust that somehow the dots will connect in the future. His story resonates with me and I often revisit it when I'm looking to pick up something new while fighting feelings of despondency over a loss or lack of form.

The path to a happy, unplanned discovery starts with learning. It doesn't matter if what you're learning now isn't of immediate relevance to the pool of resources you draw upon. In the end, these bits – the book you wanted to browse through but ended up buying, the language course you took to kill time on weekends or the guitar lessons you signed up for in college – might just come together one day, unexpectedly, beautifully, almost by accident.

Viswanathan Anand v. Joel Benjamin (1–0)
(White)   (Black)

1989 Hoogovens Tournament, Wijk aan Zee
WHITE WINS

At this point in the game, if Black recaptured my bishop after I'd played Nxd2, both my knights could attack Black's queen and it would have to be given up. I hadn't prepared this line, but suddenly a conversation I had with Vassily Ivanchuk on the Catalan opening popped up in my head and I could sense a similar pattern here in the Sicilian Defence, even though the two are quite far apart, and I executed it.

♛

Here's a lesson in serendipity and limitless learning. Nothing you do, however unconnected it is to your livelihood or your life's goal, goes waste. You never know when an idea that you've read about or heard of, or an activity you've dabbled in, will pay off. It's wise, then, to keep your interests and your learning as varied and broad as you can.

FOUR

WIN SOME, LOSE S♛ME

EMOTIONS AND THE POWER OF OBJECTIVITY

I LAY AWAKE WATCHING THE FIRST, FEEBLE SMATTERING OF daylight graze the curtains of our hotel room in Dortmund, listening to my breath rise and fall. My eyelids were heavy from the sleep my brain had adamantly put off for later, my head felt like it weighed a hundred pounds and dark swirls wound endlessly in my mind around a singular thought: I hate chess.

It was the early hours of 19 July 2001, barely a day after I'd lost to Alexander Morozevich in round 6 of the Dortmund Sparkassen Chess Meeting, and all I could think about was the grin pasted across his face as he shook my hand and thanked me for the 'birthday present' I'd served up for him. It was just seven months since my World Championship win in Tehran and here I was looking deadbeat, with three draws, two losses and almost certain to finish at the bottom. The German city with a robust chess culture was hosting six of the top 10 Super Grandmasters – Kramnik, Topalov,

Peter Leko, Morozevich, Michael Adams and me – for the invite-only double round robin tournament. The tournament was also being viewed as a test of strength for the two new world champions – Kramnik, the Brain Games champion who beat Kasparov in 2000, and me, from the FIDE cycle.

Of course, at this point I felt nothing like a Super GM. I was a mess. I couldn't eat, sleep or look at the board. I was up at 3 a.m., wondering how to kill time until the late afternoon game. This pattern had emerged over the days I had gone winless – for three games, no less – which then quickly mounted to five. By the seventh game, without a full point earned, the disturbing pattern of my anxieties hit a crescendo. I went for a walk, hit the gym, binge-watched master litigator Perry Mason salvage the stickiest situations, finished breakfast and realized I still had seven hours left to chew myself with self-loathing. It felt like the world was closing in on me.

At such moments, objectivity is the one thing you crave for. Without it a bad tournament can rapidly degenerate into a lousy one. After you've made a really bad move and the position has turned against you, the ideal response is to calm yourself and adjust to the new truth. To constantly tell yourself 'I could have won five moves ago' or 'I could have lost three moves ago' doesn't alter reality. It's a lot like making a financial investment. There's little merit in deliberating over the options that could have been exercised earlier. What matters is the worth of your existing resources. One of the methods I use to deal with a situation that looks dire for me is to step back and imagine that I've already lost the point, and see how long I can resist being affected by it.

This applies equally to good situations, when it seems every move I make is paying off. There have been instances where I've won games in which the positions suddenly became advantageous to me. I've remained unmoved, telling myself there's no hurry, that I'm going to patiently hold on to the point and not let early elation distract me.

My game against Ilya Smirin at the Intel Chess Grand Prix in 1994 in New York works as an example. Both games between us in round 1 were drawn and we were thrown into an Armageddon blitz decider. Smirin got White on a coin toss and had six minutes on the clock. I had Black, and five minutes. White needed a win, and a draw would suffice for Black to progress.

A few moves into a Petroff Defence, Smirin chose a rather unusual 4.Nxe5. What followed has now elevated the game to Internet immortality. On move four, I felt myself going numb. My clock was racing like a panther on the loose; I'd eaten up close to a minute already – unusual and unheard of in blitz games.

Smirin had captured a pawn out of sequence, which had thrown me off. I leant over the board, in my aviator-style glasses, till I could almost sniff the pieces. 'C'mon, Vishy, make a move! Make a move!' pounded the commentators, Maurice Ashley and Daniel King, impatiently (though thankfully out of my earshot). I pushed my pawn to d6, attacking White's knight and forcing it to retreat. I then wore him down with exchanges till he overreached. My decision to pause and consider had paid off – I'd gone from spending 1.43 minutes on one move to using up only two minutes on the last 46 moves and rode right into a win. It's a lesson that almost runs as a leitmotif through my career: It's not the worst idea to take a two-minute pause and get some clarity. At the board, I use the time as I see fit. If I feel like thinking deeply at one point, I follow that instinct and play faster elsewhere. Of course, the same logic doesn't quite apply if five seconds is all I have – but where it does, it pays off every time.

In Dortmund, it wasn't that I was not adequately prepared, but after two defeats – against Topalov and Morozevich – I had slipped into passive play. I was trying hard not to lose more games and was roundly whipped for it. I ended up finishing last, with three points out of a possible 10, and hit rock bottom. I couldn't do any worse, I told myself.

My winning run in tournaments through the second half of 2000 – the Frankfurt Chess Classic in June, the World Championship in New Delhi and Tehran in December that year, finishing second at the Corus Chess Tournament in Wijk aan Zee in early 2001 and winning at the Torneo Magistral Ciudad de León in Merida, Mexico, later in May – somehow ended with the worst result of my life in Dortmund. I then lost my World Championship title after being eliminated by Ivanchuk in the fourth game of our semi-final in the 128-player knockout World Championship tournament in Moscow in December 2001.

This crater I'd landed myself in wasn't entirely unexplained. Though my wins hadn't ebbed, success had masked the gaps that had crept into my game. With good results, you often shed the habit of worrying and tell yourself the wins are happening for the right reasons. You don't feel the need to identify your problem areas and work on them, because you're still raking in wins. It could well be that you are competitively strong, but your opening work is not going very well, or that your repertoire in other areas is limited. But when tension deserts you, you can no longer hear the siren going off, even when you should be attentive, alarmed and are clearly in danger. Without the red flags, the flaws go unnoticed and turn into cavernous troughs, and it's only when the tide turns that you realize you were swimming naked. Being objective at these junctures gives you the opportunity to back yourself and make changes before it comes to the point when disaster strikes.

It was at the Dubai Rapid Grand Prix in 2002 that I hit upon the road to recovery. The tournament began badly. Faster time controls were supposedly my turf, but there I was, dumped early in the second round, and shaken. A rather outlandish tournament rule that dictated that those who lost in earlier rounds had to continue to play for the final standings ended up being a godsend. I told myself I'd just turn up like none of it mattered and play without a care. I was already out of the tournament and had nothing more to lose. Remarkably, without the worry of results clamping down on my chest, I turned into my keyed-up six-year-old self and finished with as many wins (eight) as the eventual winner, Leko. I had realized that my routine needed a reshuffle so I could think and work differently from what I had been doing up until then – and I started with skipping the Wijk aan Zee tournament in early 2002, an event most unshakeably planted in my calendar over the years. Next, I struck off the Amber Tournament in Monaco from my list that year.

Further deliverance was at hand.

In the run-up to the 2002 Eurotel Trophy in Prague, I was dropped from all mentions of possible title contenders. Suddenly, it cut me loose from all the pressure. For the first time in 15 months, since Wijk aan Zee 2001, a tournament featured Kasparov, Kramnik and me in its pool of participants. In the 32-player knockout event, each match consisted of two games of 25 minutes plus five second increments for a move. In the instance of scores being tied at the end of both games, two blitz games of five minutes each with increments of two seconds per move, were to be played. If the deadlock in scores still wasn't resolved, a sudden death play-off – with five minutes for White (and a win necessary to progress) and four minutes for Black (with a draw sufficing to advance) – was contested. The final was to be played in a best-of-two-games over seven hours in the classical chess format. In the semi-finals I played Ivanchuk, who had beaten Kasparov in a sudden death tie-break in the quarter-finals. Our contest also spilled into a tie-break, which I went on to win to set up a final against Karpov before we headed into a rest day. Against Karpov, I won the first game with White to move into the lead. A draw with Black then was enough for me to haul away the title.

Motivation, I believe, ebbs and flows to its own rhythms and might have nothing to do with the effort we put into feeling it or the control we attempt to exercise over it. I've found that I've played my most inspired games when my enthusiasm for the sport resurfaced, without the bindings of titles or wins or ratings tying me down, and I've just wanted to play a good game and have been excited about learning something new or applying something fresh. There's no quick path to finding motivation, but the moment you surrender to your love for your sport – or your career or choice of activity, for that matter – is where the highest probability lies.

♛

Principally, winning in chess is centred on your emotions. It's the moments when you lose control over your emotions that decide the outcome of your games. The tactics players employ, therefore, have as much to do with progressing on the board as with drawing opponents out of their comfort zones, then lying in wait for them to wander into a mistake.

After a game I've lost or one in which I've made overwhelmingly stupid mistakes, I find myself filled with self-hatred. As the days go by, I become calmer, but every time – even weeks or months later – I think of the schoolboy error I made and what it cost me, I shudder, and the feeling surges right back. The two defeats I suffered against Wang Hao in 2013 (at Wijk aan Zee and the Norway Chess tournament) still bother me. These results influenced my play in the tournaments that followed and anytime I got into a technical position, I would start anticipating my mistakes and worrying about a loss, which would then affect both my game and my equilibrium.

When you see tennis players furious at themselves, after they've lost a point perhaps or right after an unfavourable umpire call, beating their rackets against the court, you realize they are venting their frustration, but their mood isn't really improving. In fact, that kind of violent channelling only makes it worse. In football too, if a national team botches up a chance in the ninetieth minute, everyone in the team carries the wound for a long time. They may put it aside and part ways temporarily to play for their respective clubs, but they'll only heal from the memory of that loss if they win in a similar situation when they're back playing for the national side. The mind only recovers emotionally when it can replace an old memory with a new, more pleasant one.

Similarly, when things are going badly in chess, I've found that not only does it help to identify the sticky areas and change things around, but it also pays to completely change my surroundings, find something new and compelling, and shift attention away from the low points for at least a short while.

After a bad game I tend to find myself in the gym, running. When I'm on the treadmill, I feel the anger like a raw nerve and the first thing that flashes in my mind when I get off it is that the loss is real, still fresh and hurting, and the memory of it hasn't gone away. But I'm sweating, perhaps slightly exhausted, so I go for a shower, eat and then doze off, and the next morning I always wake up feeling better.

The World Championship match between Kasparov and Karpov in Seville in 1987 offered me a profound lesson in objectivity. Here was the world's greatest player, Kasparov, trailing 11–12 in the match, but instead of striking his head against the washboard over his predicament, he spent the entire night playing cards. He had realized that he wasn't going to come up with answers overnight. Giving yourself time to recover emotionally is worth a lot more than the flash of a great idea. You may have the best preparation in place but if you're emotionally distraught it's unlikely you'll be able to summon up the means or the will to execute any of it. On match day, Kasparov woke up in the afternoon, had a late, lazy lunch and headed to the tournament hall telling himself he was just going to keep it going, maintain enough pieces on the board and play decent chess. He and his team hadn't worked every line to its end, but had chalked out a few starting points in every line so that he could improvise, add a touch of creativity on the board and the chance of his blundering into something wholly unknown was minimum.

I've followed that approach often. Sometimes I tell myself I'll improvise in one area, and riff in another. The aim is not to cover my opponent's most likely line of play but loosely cover the eight or nine possibilities that may arise, leaving little margin for error. I managed to, in fact, employ it against Karpov during our 1998 World Championship match in Lausanne. In game 6, I was certain he was looking for a draw. I came up with the unusual Trompowsky, an aggressive and tricky opening that leads to non-standard positions early on, and Karpov overstepped his game.

♛

No matter what you may be feeling emotionally, being inscrutable at the board is a vital skill.

I'm not someone who's easily given to expressing emotions, but to players who know me well, the tiniest, seemingly imperceptible gestures I make can come across as coded messages conveying panic, shock, joy or plain grief. Many players like to bluff and display an exaggerated sense of confidence or even anger at themselves for making a mistake, all the while masking their true emotions. It's a form of active deception. I prefer the uncomplicated path of doing neither. I just hunker down and reveal as little as possible. Perhaps my biggest giveaway in a tense scenario is chewing my nails. A friend of mine once told me – and I see his point here – that biting your nails is almost like going to war with yourself. If I've blundered or sensed that I'm on my way to making a hash of things, my nails will be gone quite quickly. I'm aware it's a visible cue for my opponent, and I've managed to successfully control this habit over the years in some measure, but I can't seem to be able to help it as an instinctive response.

Among my opponents, when Kramnik, for instance, is in a tight spot, he sometimes suddenly plays aggressively, attacking out of desperation, and I can tell he's lost the positional battle and is now pretending that everything is part of the plan. I also pick up on his fidgeting at times, but he is a person who is habitually fidgety, so one has to intuitively tell apart the movements that arise out of nervousness and those that are natural. Kasparov is quite the master at putting up an act – scowling, glaring and glowering – and he does it rather well because he's an actor who believes in his character and he knows it unsettles the person sitting across him. But the reason his theatrics work is that he's a great player. Without that essential quality, intimidation tactics would be hard to pull off or made to look believable. Unlike many others, Carlsen can be quite difficult to read, because he can look both uninterested and confident at the same time. During the 2019 Grand Chess Tour in Croatia, I played a Ke3 move against him and then looked at him to see if I had guaged his thoughts correctly. My move had improved my position dramatically, but when I couldn't be sure of his response I began to look for clues that would reveal if he had seen something I hadn't. Finally, when he spent the next 25 minutes poring over it, I was more than certain that he had missed it. I told myself that even if I lost the position, it was at least going to be a much harder win than he'd thought. We went on to draw that game.

Very often, a few moves before your opponent makes a blunder, you can sense things begin to curdle. It's inexplicable. It's the kind of intuition that possibly comes from a heightened sense of awareness of the space around you. It's hard to simulate that while training at home. As a marker of giveaways, breathing patterns are what I watch for most in my opponents. They might look completely placid after having committed a howler, but a wavering breath might be the clue I'm looking for. I've harnessed this technique to my benefit often when opponents with faces like that of standing water suddenly hold their breath after a move. It sets me off on a hunt and there, right there, lying sprawled before me is my opponent's blunder and my opportunity at cutting off any retreat for his king.

In spite of my natural propensity to stay away from conflict, when I look back now, I feel there were certain moments in my life when I could have been more confrontational. At the Dortmund tournament in 1997, Karpov came in 40 minutes late for a game against me. He was perhaps trying to push his luck, attempting to unsettle me and get away with it. I had already guessed the possible sequence of events when he didn't show up five minutes past the start time, and anticipated that the arbiter would be spineless about the transgression. Just as I'd expected, once Karpov arrived, instead of applying the rules, the arbiter turned to me, expecting me to make a request for action to be taken. Karpov offered the excuse that he didn't get his taxi in time, which of course I didn't believe. I had two choices here – to cry foul, or to move on with the game. I remember considering if the lost time would really help – the kind of objectivity the brain offers when you want to avoid conflict – all the while incensed at the arbiter for not being assertive. In the end, I asked him to give Karpov his time back and we got on with the game. To me, squabbling and haranguing in such pre-game scenarios seems like a waste; it implies I'm diverting and expending the energy I would otherwise use to mentally revise my preparatory notes.

I would say I'm a bit of an anomaly among the group of players I've belonged to over the years. In a similar scenario, Kramnik might not have thrown a tantrum, but he would have made his displeasure known, Kasparov would never accept decisions he didn't approve of, and Carlsen wouldn't have been consenting of it either.

In a way, I vicariously enjoy watching people stand their ground. I used to be fascinated by Nieves's doughty spirit, which had her bearing down on hotel staff who went back on a booking, or calling up high-ranking government officials to expedite visa procedures for me. I marvelled at the recent instance of Carlsen's refusal to play the 2020 World Championship in Stavanger, Norway, to avoid the attendant crushing pressure of defending his World Championship title on home soil.

    Being confrontational can hardly be a one-off affair. It's a ceaseless loop. You have to keep clarifying your position and stick to it. There are people who thrive in an atmosphere of combat, tension and conflict – but that has never been my strongest suit. Generally, my best results come when I'm happy and my mind isn't preoccupied with external diversions. This has perhaps often led people to assume I'm a pushover. I suppose I suit the 'nice guy' stereotype rather perfectly, with my tucked-in monochrome shirts, neatly parted hair and generally non-confrontational manner. When my favourite footballer, Zinedine Zidane, charged like a bull on the Pamplona run and head-butted Italy's Marco Materazzi in his sternum at the FIFA World Cup final in 2006, I wasn't filled with consternation. I felt it was an act that had to be seen in its context. I often wrestle with the thought of standing up to obnoxious behaviour. Yet, whatever the provocation, after I've run it through the sieve of objectivity, I know I wouldn't be comfortable with hostility or retaliation. I'm quite clear that if I win I'd have already shut people up with my performance, and if I lose there's no point in going over the rough patches – the ones outside my own performance, that is – again. Screaming injustice afterwards, especially in sport, is pointless, because you're just seen as a whiner. I prefer to focus on being ruthlessly objective, tell myself my aim is to see my next two games through and move on.

At times, though, when I've faced challenges off the board, it is chess that has emerged as therapy.

The Norway Chess tournament of June 2015 offered a measure of timely catharsis to a particularly painful personal loss – my mother's death. On 26 May that year, I was on a break in Chennai between tournaments, when my parents' residence number flashed on my phone at 1.18 a.m. My heart sank. Aruna and my son, Akhil, then five years old, were asleep beside me. I ran out of the room to answer the call and heard my father at the other end of the line trying to sound collected and unalarmed. My mother, he told me, was not waking up despite his repeated attempts at rousing her, and asked if I would be able to come over. Aruna was awake by then and we knew it could be what we were dreading. I called for an ambulance and got myself a cab. The ride to my parents' home, five kilometres away, took just over five minutes. I reached around the same time as the paramedics and we rushed to the bedroom on the first floor. A few minutes later, the medics confirmed that my mother had passed away in her sleep over two hours ago. This was a kind of loss I'd never faced before – and one, I realized, I was thoroughly unprepared for.

I went through the customary mourning period of 13 days mostly in a daze, surrounded by people at all times. There was no opportunity for me to grieve. Most of the time, I was glad to be involved in conversations that took my mind off what had just happened, silently wondering why extended families always waited for such sombre occasions to meet instead of getting together more often. Almost by chance, the rituals concluded the day before I was to leave for

Norway, and it was only when I sat in the flight, fastened my seat belt and felt the wheels of the aircraft whizzing down the runway that my loss hit me with a sense of finality. I was wracked with guilt, wondering if there was anything more I could have done for my mother when she had been around and thinking of all the things I'd left unsaid. I cried uncontrollably on the flight.

Once I reached Stavanger and was by myself in my hotel room, I broke down again. Contrary to my hope that physical distance from Chennai, its familiar streets, the rooms in our house filled with my mother's scent and everything else that reminded me of her would help lessen the pain, I ended up crying every single day. I tried to expend all my energy at the board during the games so that I was left with little or no vitality by the end of the day, and could just collapse into bed and drift off to sleep. I had a fantastic tournament, almost good enough to finish in first place. Had Topalov not had such a terrific outing, I'd have run away with it. I found myself in no serious crisis throughout the event and played out a short draw against him in just half an hour in the final round. Still, finishing second, half a point behind him, was heartening. At the end of it, I felt partially healed.

The only other time I've felt myself crumble for reasons other than a loss at the chessboard was 11 years before my mother's death, in November 2004, when Aruna gave me the news of the loss of our unborn child. This was eight years after our marriage, when both our families were anxiously waiting for us to become parents. I had just finished playing the Corsica Masters then. The previous month, I'd left for the

Chess Olympiad FIDE had organized in Calvià, flush with the news of a baby's arrival in our lives, having excitedly registered myself on an American website that would allow me to record and track the progression of the pregnancy right up to the birth. Aruna had suffered the miscarriage soon after I'd left, but had kept the news from me so that I wouldn't be distracted by it mid-tournament. I recall my hand freezing when I heard the news, and when I spoke, my voice choked up as I attempted to string together a coherent response. We agreed that a child would always be a happy addition to our lives, but if it didn't happen nothing would change between us. Seven years after the incident and 15 years into our marriage, in April 2011, we became parents when our son was born.

♛

Over the years, my preferred way of dealing with unattended emotions when I'm angry, sad or annoyed has been to go for long walks. I can walk across cities, countries and continents, and not be able to tell if I have gone past the first bend from our home.

I remember the time I'd dropped to two losses in a row to Teimour Radjabov and Victor Bologan at the Dortmund tournament in 2003, and strode out for a walk, seething at myself. Aruna walked quietly beside me, struggling to maintain pace. 'Have nothing to say?' I'd snapped at her. 'Normally, you have a lot of advice to give.'

Aruna didn't respond, perhaps aware that nothing she said was going to placate me. After I'd nagged her enough for a response, she replied, 'Tomorrow will be better; maybe you should try breathing deeply.'

We were about to cross the road and I remember stopping there, awfully annoyed. 'Is this the best advice you can give? Tell me if you have something against the Berlin opening.' Aruna was now angry too, and rightly so. She hadn't wanted to offer a comment in the first place and I'd pushed her into doing so. 'If I knew of something against the Berlin, do you think I would be married to you?' she retorted. Cars whizzed past us as we stood on the sidewalk, looking at each other, suddenly wondering why we were angry. We burst out laughing and that detonated the fuse that was waiting to go off in my head.

Bottling up emotions, even if done bit by bit, one tiny instance after another, can cumulatively turn into a giant, unwieldy heap of rocks you can no longer tow. You just keep pushing down the angst, pretending nothing has happened, but the truth is it's going nowhere. If you bury it for too long, the collection of repressed emotions will simmer and eventually boil over in a fiercer form, often at the most ill-timed moments when you can barely afford it.

Ilya Smirin v. Viswanathan Anand (0–1)
(White)   (Black)

1994 Intel Chess Grand Prix, Active (blitz), New York
BLACK WINS

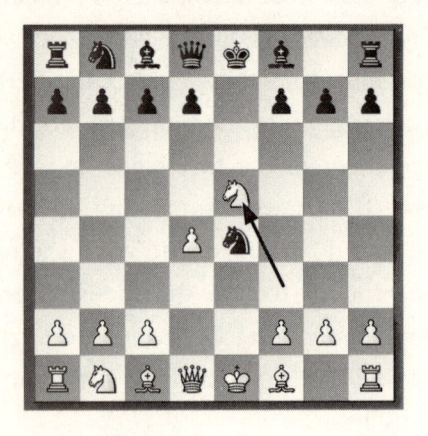

Against Smirin, on move 4, I suddenly drew a blank. The normal move would be to attack his knight, but I was worried about him making a capture at f7. I sat there, mulling over my next move, aware of the clock ticking away. My hand was unwilling to move until my mind found a path. Looking back, taking the time to think calmly through my next moves, even while pressured for time, turned out to be a good decision.

♕

Emotions tend to get in the way of clear thinking. Whether it's impatience, frustration, fury, self-loathing or even premature elation – allowing these to consume the mind results in a loss of focus and distraction from learning, and keeps you from taking the right decisions and achieving your goal. Training your mind to take a step back at the crucial moment and developing cues to organize your thoughts is more advantageous than making a move while your mind is in turmoil.

FIVE

GA♞HERING THE TROOPS

HOW TO MAKE PREPARATION COUNT AND TACTICS WORK

I REMEMBER A CONVERSATION WITH KEN THOMPSON, ONE OF THE inventors of the UNIX operating system and B programming language, both path-breaking foundations of present-day computing. This was in 1998, around the time computers were surpassing us at making tactical moves, but it was universally agreed then that humans were much better at strategy. On being asked if computers would ever catch up with humans in strategy, Thompson's response was, 'Of course! Strategy is just long-term tactics.' It was an intriguing observation and over time I have come to realize its proximity to the truth.

Chess is 99 per cent tactics. If you don't pay attention to the tactics, no strategy you devise will fetch you rewards. Strategy can't compensate for mistakes in execution. If you persist with neat execution, it will keep you in the game even if you're not able to follow a broader strategy. Strategy without tactics, though, falls at the first hurdle. For me, strategizing for a game isn't about putting together a specific manoeuvre of pieces. It's about thinking what my opponent could be aiming for, knowing what my objectives are and then preparing to get what I want out of the game.

Strategy is one of those nice words in chess that are hard to implement. You have to approach a problem systematically, but as a part of something larger. There should be a framework and, to the extent feasible, details have to fit into the concept, which then brings about harmony.

In most sports, coaches can be seen pacing the sidelines, cheering, hooting and hollering at their players. By contrast, chess players have an invisible army at work, tucked away from public view, putting their sleep and often their own careers on hold, and grinding in bottomless hours of preparatory work. For my first Candidates match against Alexey Dreev in 1991, I had Ferdinand Hellers, a Swedish friend from the junior circuit, and John van der Wiel, whom I had met many times before, as my trainers. They were good friends of mine, which was helpful since it was the first time that I was working in any sort of organized fashion. The Swedes didn't have the Soviet chess culture and Hellers was self-taught and incredible at studying the game. We were of the same age and his highly methodical opening preparation allowed me to assemble my work in a much more efficient way than I would have managed on my own. Van der Wiel brought a lot of experience to our tiny working group. He was older than us and had, in his native Holland, played several competitions, including games against Karpov a few times. It added a practical perspective to my preparation. This kind of training was more than sufficient for my first Candidates match in Madras, which Hellers attended, and I was happy to have passed the initial test.

Once I learnt that I was to face Karpov for the Candidates quarter-finals in Brussels, I began to deliberate upon the ideal team for the match. My seconds from the Dreev match had other commitments to attend to. Hellers wanted to study law and Van der Wiel was also otherwise occupied. I too had the feeling that I might need to work with someone who had a greater understanding of Karpov's thought processes and could take my training up a notch. There was no way I could afford to add another member to the existing team then.

A mutual friend suggested the Soviet player Mikhail Gurevich, who had worked with Kasparov for the World Championship match against Karpov in Seville, 1987. Gurevich, who'd moved to Brussels that year, was looking for work opportunities and was glad to hop on board. Hiring his services was expensive, but I recognized his worth because he was capable of doing a lot of work single-handedly. What struck me when we sat down for our first training camp was that nothing shook him from a task till he had completed it. One of the first things he did as my second was take away my Walkman.

Gurevich was thoroughly professional, arriving punctually at my rented accommodation which was close to where he lived, working through the day and leaving right on time. He was a brilliant second and I felt that my opening preparation improved vastly in quality during the time we worked together. Whenever we got together, we built up a bank of ideas that I could live on for the next few months. We went over Karpov's games and Gurevich helped me comprehend his ability to maintain tension at the board, wring the opponent dry of mental reserves and force errors. Rather than seeing his own plan through, Karpov's primary focus, Gurevich had analysed, largely centered on what his opponent wanted and how he could be stopped. It sounds dramatic and hard to put into practice, but sitting at the board, mentally flipping the board every once a while and trying to imagine what your opponent would want to do can be a useful exercise – even if it doesn't produce a result. My fear going into the match was of looking like someone who had stepped out of his league, but Gurevich's insights were timely, and in that match I was incredibly effective in blocking Karpov. In the end, though, I found Karpov's resistance exceedingly high and I struggled to score from winning positions. He would defend endlessly and, eventually, I couldn't hold up.

Gurevich's smoking habit soon turned into a deal-breaker between us. He was also an active player at the time, so that tension too played itself out in the backdrop. He needed to light up often while we worked, and the smell and the smoke tended to clutter my head. I couldn't live with it and he couldn't live without it. It was the kind of problem that just couldn't be fixed, so we decided to part ways.

In the early 1990s, when I was living in Maurice and Nieves's home in Spain, Georgian Grandmaster Elizbar Ubilava, who'd previously worked with Karpov, visited them. In the years that Gurevich and I were working together, between 1991 and 1993, I largely travelled on my own for tournaments. Once we ended our association, Nieves suggested I hire a full-time second, who could also accompany me for tournaments.

Ubilava had just moved to Madrid then and had the kind of deep experience I lacked. He promptly agreed to my offer, and in 1994, one year before my World Championship match against Kasparov, we formalized our working relationship. Ubilava complemented me beautifully and had the most exceptional ability to look for unconventional moves, the kind that did not easily strike me. In every position, his first idea was to think of something totally unusual and out of the box. Normally at the board I don't look to execute crazy moves, and I'm impressed by those who can play the kind of positions that I don't have the patience to pursue. Ubilava's insights lent my thinking the kind of creativity that I lacked during home analysis – I tended to work in a dogmatic fashion during training although at the board I could ideate and improvise. He also shared with me anecdotes from Karpov's life, the ones that make you realize that even the seemingly mighty champions have their foibles. In many ways, the quality of my work levelled up several notches during our time together, until we went our separate ways in the early 2000s. With each of my trainers, my preparatory ideas and methods moved ahead to fresh, new squares.

In addition to such collaborative work, another method that has helped me get invaluable insights was rifling through the experiences of former greats. In 2001, when my results hit a trough and I was struggling to find a way back, I started buying old chess books in the hope that they would rekindle ideas and help me refine my thoughts. I scanned through the collected games of Alexander Alekhine, Emanuel Lasker and José Raúl Capablanca, and it struck me how modern many of their games looked, almost like games played in the 1990s. Capablanca was a particularly difficult opponent and Alekhine hadn't come close to beating him until their World Championship match in 1927. While preparing for the match, Alekhine decided he needed to pay close and meticulous attention to Capablanca's games. He knew that without that kind of study, he would be blown to pieces. From the games he pored over he distilled two learnings. First, that he could not afford to be afraid of Capablanca's strongest suit, which was playing clear, simple positions. He decided to train harder and better, so he was equipped to confront Capablanca in his areas of strength and was not always forced to duck or hide when the latter made his moves. He also delved into the kind of positions Capablanca didn't particularly excel at and probed them. The match, which Alekhine went on to win, became one of the most famous chess games in history and it's hard to ignore how unlikely the final outcome had seemed earlier, given his former dismal record against Capablanca.

Ahead of his 1961 World Championship rematch against reigning champion Mikhail Tal, Mikhail Botvinnik put in hours of work, going over his opponent's games and trying to look for ways around it so he didn't feel totally helpless later. The barrier for Botvinnik was largely psychological. At the board, Tal's moves were not about difficulty of calculation; rather, they revolved around intimidating the opponent's mind. His approach involved posing a plethora of tactical problems. The truth is, very few players like to defend against too many pieces or be weighed down by calculations while battling the lurking fear of something going wrong. Botvinnik prepared by playing training games in exactly that kind of maelstrom and moving into openings that would neutralize Tal's threats if not eliminate them.

For a modern player to cull lessons from great games of past masters, just reading about them or watching them is not enough. To get the most out of this kind of knowledge, it is useful to visualize the situation the player faced while studying the game. Only if you can place yourself in that situation can you benefit in any way; otherwise it ends up feeling like a mystery novel you've already read and know the ending of. You can then no longer summon up the excitement to explore further.

♛

Though established theory is burgeoning, in chess the objective is always to overturn it and draw your opponent out of the safety zone and into the combat arena. The approach you take to do this depends on the kind of player you are.

Essentially, there are two types of players – those with a horizontal approach and those who subscribe to a vertical path. A horizontal player can be likened to a banyan tree. Much like the expansive tree, they have a broad understanding, are able to respond to each stimulus and provocation differently, and even move laterally between systems, making for versatile play. It's tougher to plan an ambush against such a player since you can never be sure where you'll find them on the board. Vertical players, on the other hand, go down a straight path, trekking deeper into variations, scouring for nuances that could make a difference, and can be compared to a palm tree.

Each has its pros and each its cons, and you don't have to pick one or the other approach. In fact, I believe most players eventually gravitate to the approach that suits them best. It is, however, worth trying both because you can't be certain which will work best for you, not just as a player but against various opponents and different formats. The horizontal path teaches you diversity and flexibility, while the vertical approach is about delving deeper into a problem and not just addressing it superficially. Using a combination of both and trying to strike the ideal balance could lead one to the golden mean. The exact mix that suits each player is hard to find, though it's clear that it's unlikely to be a convenient 50:50.

There are players who can dabble in both at the same time, and I too have done that often. It's not so much an advantage as a choice. It's easier for me to be focused and narrow against a single player, but when I'm playing a tournament this approach will not cut ice. There are obdurate players who stick to playing one line throughout their career, but that may pose difficulties in the current chess scenario where you need to be able to play a variety of opponents, since the tournaments are structured in such a way that you could be facing a teenage Grandmaster or a veteran in almost any game. The trick may lie in preparing broadly and, closer to the game, narrowing your preparation to five options. From this, you could select the two you are most likely to encounter, focus heavily on them and disregard the rest. But if your opponent is the kind of player who outperforms with surprises, then instead of obsessing over one aspect it's practical to spread yourself thin with a minimum level of preparation in all areas. Either way, you have the choice of going deep or broad, and you can pick whatever increases your odds the most.

As with any learning process, in chess too you have to be curious about areas you don't know about – that is, the openings and systems you don't play or believe you need – because you cannot foresee when an opportunity to use them will present itself. Without that spirit of inquiry, you completely lose the ability to be opportunistic. I've found that the best players are the ones who are the most curious.

Curiosity fuels your mind and spreads your knowledge base, which inevitably expands your repertoire, makes you flexible and agile, allows you to adapt and promptly respond to changing circumstances, and increases the chances of serendipity coming to your aid. Almost every chess player evolves through their playing days in this way. In fact, I would go so far as to say that any player who doesn't train himself to be flexible right from his days as a junior competitor will run into problems later. Sometimes you may come across opponents who have the ability to neutralize your strengths, and if you can't switch mid-stream you might lose.

This is not just true of chess – even in your everyday roles, say in your career or with your skill set, being narrow can be self-defeating. If your particular expertise or function is suddenly fulfilled by artificial intelligence or automation, or outsourced to another company, and you're in the uncomfortable situation of not possessing any other domain knowledge or skills, it's a lot harder to shift and adapt to the change. There are those who may even be unable to change the way they do their jobs – which puts them in serious trouble. A microcosm of this is seen in chess, in the openings, schemes, middle games, structures and endgames. Twenty years ago, you could still get by as a vertical player. Now, it's just impossible.

A spirit of inquiry also comes in handy when studying positions you dislike playing – the ones that don't suit your style, for instance. In my own case, dry positions, or the ones in which the tension in the position has disappeared, turning them lifeless, vex me. Carlsen, on the contrary, uses dry, bloodless positions brilliantly to his advantage, playing dead drawn endings, navigating into complexity and hatching fresh threats until his opponent cracks. He employed this strategy against me at the 2013 World Championship, and I ended up losing my title. You can start by asking yourself a few questions: What goes wrong at the board in this position? Why is it that my focus dips and I end up making a blunder when I reach this point? When you adopt such a learning method, even a boring and depressing position can become interesting. Additionally, you can throw yourself tiny challenges. For instance, tell yourself, 'Let me see if in today's training session I can defend this kind of technical position well.' This involves diving into your own mind and its machinations, and you have to be truly objective and honest with yourself for such an exercise to be fruitful. Your aim is to see if you're getting the same negative vibes when rehearsing the position at home as you get during a game. If you are, then you will be successful in dealing with it later. But if you don't get to the bottom of why it's going wrong at the board, why you dislike the position to begin with, then it may not work.

Beyond value judgements of positions, the deeper you trudge into the details of preparatory work, the more confident you will feel, which in turn raises the probability of your success. At the board, your job is to win. The process you follow to do this, the improvements you make, your consistency till the end of the game, the way you play middle games, apply your preparation and analyse your learning – all of it makes you the player you are and decides games for you.

For instance, after I've calculated a long, beautiful line for which I've travelled deep and uncovered interesting facets, I always return to the first move and run an error check. I don't have to see the whole line then, but just look for the missing gaps. The longer the line, the more the chances of making a mistake. Often, in trying to look for beauty, I find I've missed something elementary. More crucially, I ensure that the error-checking process stands apart from my thought process while making the moves. That is, instead of simply looking closely for what I may have missed, I look for what I may have been inattentive to in similar positions in the past, what other players typically neglect in these kinds of positions, the examples of actual games I can think of related to the line or position, and force myself to remain mindful of mental blocks that have earlier led to obvious mistakes.

Often, when both sides are deadlocked, I find some

unutilized resource – a pawn or a knight stuck at the other end of the board – suddenly stirring into participation and deciding the game. Many of these moves involving the last piece can be incredibly beautiful, and a certain sense of justice prevails over this resource holding the answer that you were looking for. In my game against Alexander Beliavsky at the 1993 PCA qualifiers in Groningen, I was faced with the choice of opting for a clever side line, which may have fallen off his match preparation, over sticking to the main line. Through most of my career, I have done the smart thing and assumed there was some nasty surprise waiting for me and then gone the other way. In this case, though, perhaps it was the buoyancy of youth that got me charging into the main line. It paid off spectacularly. I found a move on the board which posed arduous problems for Black. I hadn't consciously aimed for this position and executed it in my typical way, allowing myself to enter an opening and confronting it. In that instance, my curiosity drove me to take on the risks. In life as well, some underutilized resource you may possess, might be the element to bring into play in a difficult situation. The key then is self-knowledge – a deep awareness of the resources you possess, whether you're actively using them or not.

For tournaments, I may prepare three openings but end up surviving the length of the event on just two. In the first game I may play the defence I want, in the second I may repeat it, and just when my opponents get a grip on it and plan to waylay me the next time, I switch.

Certain situations may also require you to take risks that you're not 100 per cent sure of. I've had both kinds of experiences – ones in which I've decided on moves at the last minute and they've paid off like a dream, and those in which I've played moves I know little about in depth and ended up crash-landing. The best method is, of course, to have a little surprise up your sleeve. You may know a few bits of it and what you're up against, and decide to assume the risk – but you need to have some tolerance of the fact that you may not know all the details yourself. Naturally, whatever you embark on shouldn't be completely random, such as positions and ideas that you know absolutely nothing about. You want to surprise your opponent and shouldn't end up surprising yourself. There needs to be a starting point, some work done at the base so that when you want to do something totally different at the board, when you want to improvise and find your way around new situations, you're not starting at zero. When you have even the slightest bit of preparation, you can look at shifting the odds in your favour. I have been at the other end of surprises too. A classic example of this is the Dragon, which Kasparov used against me during our 1995 World Championship match. The Dragon is a variation of the Sicilian which draws its name from the resemblance of the Black kingside pawn structure to the Draco constellation in the northern sky, also known as the Dragon. It typically fianchettoes a bishop on the h6-a1 diagonal. Kasparov's use of it caught me completely off guard in game 11, which led me to make a blunder and I lost the game. He brought it back again in game 13 and though I had a good idea of it by then I managed to mess up my responses, make screaming mistakes and was lost. Suddenly, the Dragon, which I could have negotiated, looked like a stroke of genius. It ended up working much better than it should have because of its surprise value and the psychological effect it had on me.

It doesn't always have to be about executing an attack; sometimes even the threat of an attack can prove to be more effective than the actual execution. At a technical level, I would stash away a manoeuvre in reserve till the circumstances demanded that I bring it forth. The point is to mess with the opponent's mind. Just dangling a threat, like veering forces towards the enemy king, has more effect because it's much harder for most people to contend with an ambiguous hazard than a specific danger they need to respond to. It causes them to lose focus while running through the possibilities of an unknown attack.

I've found that while striving for perfection, immersing yourself completely in a line or an idea is a useful learning method, it can also be a handicap in certain circumstances. This is true especially if you're up against very practical players. With them, you have to have a sense of when they are making a good move and when they are bluffing. At a certain point in the game, you may have to respond to your gut telling you that you don't want to be the one to make the last mistake – that moving away from the need to make a perfect move is the prudent response. This learning can be extrapolated to other areas of life as well. Striving for perfection as a means of self-improvement is valid, but if you have a deadline to meet or an emergent situation to deal with, it's probably the worst occasion to try to be perfect. The conflict within arises because a part of you wants to be perfect, but the other part, the voice of reason, knows that you have neither the time nor the resources to do so then.

Before a game, I've found that training for short bursts can be as effective as trying to work for a long time, especially when it comes to intense work where you absolutely block all distractions and focus on the problem. If you work for a long time, then inevitably, at some point, your mind will wander, and your energy and interest will both flag. You may end up squandering your resources. Short bursts, I've found, are the most productive – much like brief meetings, or indeed short working days – because they can be intense, focused periods when you stop thinking of everything else and quit multi-tasking. Naturally, when your work interests you, you're able to work a lot harder during the short bursts. The best concentration exercise you can give yourself is working on something that really intrigues you. In areas you find unpleasant, setting yourself mini targets might be helpful.

While it's supremely important to concentrate during a game, it's equally important to not concentrate the whole time. Of course, this is only possible when you have some time in hand and are not counting down seconds. After the little break you've allowed yourself, you consciously need to be able to snap out of it, get back into game mode and focus on the board before making a move. At times, when I'm in a troubling position, I let my mind wander and think about Monty Python's Holy Grail and the limbless knight or an absurd scene from *Yes Minister*. It lightens my mood and is a pleasant diversion. If there's time and it's my opponent's turn to play, I walk around for a bit rather than racking my brain over the five possible moves he could make. Sometimes, odd tunes play in a loop in my head, like Akhil's nursery rhyme 'Pat a Cake', which I couldn't stop humming during one of the tie-break games at the 2012 World Championship tournament against Gelfand.

♛

Routine is another crucial aspect of preparation. It may appear to be the not-so-flashy facet, but following a routine is really about discipline and focus. If you stick to a routine, you can save a lot of energy on a whole host of things and you are able to think when you're at the board. Famously, Steve Jobs's choice of a turtleneck as everyday workwear, as with Mark Zuckerberg's grey T-shirt, left him with one less thing to think about in the morning and more time to ideate on running a successful and growing business.

When it comes to routines, the equivalent of a tennis player being finicky about his racket or a cricketer over the grip of his bat for me would be reaching the city where I'm scheduled to play a tournament a couple of days early. I walk around its streets, look out for food joints and try some of them out – it's the way I condition and familiarize myself with the venue, so I'm comfortable and settled in by the time the match begins. It may have nothing to do with being boxed into a room, feeling the breath of my opponent on me, but it puts my mind at ease, almost as if to suggest that the surprises are out of the way.

There are aspects of my routine which are far removed from strategy or logic – perhaps even sanity – but have fought and wormed their way into my schedule and have stayed. The shirts I wear to matches, for instance. I'm not too fussed about them, but it may be hard for me to overlook that a part of my wardrobe may have outperformed the rest of it. I have a black shirt with red stripes and a white collar that could easily walk away with the honours for the Most Valuable Player. I wore it when I beat Aronian and Topalov and drew Sergey Karjakin to qualify at the 2014 Candidates in Khanty-Mansiysk. The first thought that floated into my head was, 'Wow, that's a lethal one!' Incidentally, I'd also worn it when I'd defeated Aronian a year earlier at Wijk aan Zee, in what was one of my best games of all time, and during some of my winning performances in 2007. I can't deny, though, that it's easy to remember only the good times and think, 'Oh, this is my luckiest shirt,' and forget about the times I've lost while wearing it. In Riyadh, at the World Rapid & Blitz Chess Championship in 2017, I gave up on this kind of thinking. I'd run through all the shirts I had packed for the tournament and my results didn't look up until later.

    I can get quite obsessive about the little things. There are certain pens I've used once or twice for match notes, and I want to use them repeatedly, or I switch pens for my Black and White games alternately and stick to that routine. Sometimes, I'll be sitting for breakfast thinking that if I don't have an omelette I may lose the game, or if I eat something extra it will cost me a point. It would be silly to think that any of this could have a bearing on what I end up doing at the board, but before a game the mind is always scanning for familiar external patterns or routines as cues for comfort. I suppose every situation where the outcome is important rouses the irrational in human beings. The actual cause and effect is less significant than the apprehension that brings such thoughts to mind.

In the absence of a routine, or engagements that fill gaps between games, if I spend my time engaging in random activity, it goes badly for me. There have been several rapid and blitz events that have gone disastrously for me – in Berlin in 2015, where I finished twenty-fifth in the rapid (and twenty-second in the blitz) and Doha in 2016, where I ended in sixteenth place in the rapid, for instance. The pairings were very slow in coming, the hall was too small for the number of participants and it was crowded, so I found myself hanging around aimlessly between games. With nothing constructive to do, looking for someone to talk to or idly strolling around is far from an ideal scenario, because it slowly turns your mind vapid. To avoid a similar situation later, at Riyadh in 2017, where I went on to win the rapid title, I carried my laptop to the venue so that I could sit somewhere and solve puzzles, or even watch something just to avoid walking around feeling aimless. It worked superbly. Riyadh was brilliantly organized too, so I had a chair to sit in between rounds. It may not have been an option in other tournaments. When it comes to routines, you have to find the balance between what you want to do and what's possible in a particular situation.

Viswanathan Anand v. Alexander Beliavsky (1-0)
(White) (Black)

1993 PCA Qualifiers, Groningen
WHITE WINS

It may have just been the optimism of youth, but I decided to charge into a line which Beliavsky could have been well prepared to play. It paid off brilliantly. I discovered a move which poses difficult problems for Black. I did it in my typical way, submerging myself in the opening and, then, once it was too late to come back, confronting it and giving it all I had.

♛

For your strategy to be effective, the preparation you put into every aspect to make your tactics work efficiently is key. Your approach cannot be unidimensional. Whether you're taking in external perspectives, keeping your mind open to varied sources of learning, visualizing difficult, unknown scenarios and tackling them head-on through practice, cultivating discipline and a routine that brings you comfort in the face of stressful situations – all of it eventually comes together to contribute to the moment of achievement.

SIX

NEW YORK, NEW Y♛RK

THE MAKING OF A CHAMPION

IN THE DINING AREA OF OUR HOTEL IN WIJK AAN ZEE, WHERE WE'D landed for the annual tournament in January 1998, Karpov sat at the table ahead of us, within earshot, nodding to a journalist's queries. A question cropped up on the World Championship match we'd played against each other – that Karpov had won – in Lausanne just a week earlier. As a corollary to it, there came a query on my future prospects of being a World Champion. 'Ah, well, Vishy's a nice guy,' Karpov remarked with a happy snort, 'but he just doesn't have the character for a big win.'

Aruna, seated beside me, had also caught the snide remark. She dug her fork into her bowl of fruit and we ate the rest of our meal in silence. His words had hit a raw nerve. It was a decidedly unpleasant feeling to be seen as a good player who lacked the conviction to win big.

The bland 'nice guy' label had stuck to me ever since the Professional Chess Association (PCA) World Championship match against Kasparov at the Observation Deck of the World Trade Center in New York in September 1995.

That match stood out in my mind for many reasons. For one thing, I hadn't learnt of its venue being shifted from the originally designated German city of Cologne to the 107th floor of the New York skyscraper until I'd already booked rooms at the former location for myself and my team of four seconds – my then trainer Ubilava; Patrick Wolff; Jon Speelman, formerly part of Nigel Short's battery of seconds during his 1993 match against Kasparov; and Artur Yusupov, who'd worked with me during the Candidates final against Gata Kamsky in Las Palmas in the lead-up to the Kasparov match. We'd thrown ourselves into a three-month-long camp in my Madrid home, sparring and obsessing over my first shot at the World Championship title.

Then, two months before the championship in September, the original prize fund of $1.5 million was slashed by 10 per cent, ostensibly to cover the 'organizational costs' of the PCA. The conditions stipulated that two-thirds of the money would go to the winner, and in case the match was tied, Kasparov would retain the PCA World Champion title and the prize money would be split between us. The rules and the turf belonged to Kasparov. I wasn't consulted on any of the decisions. It was almost as though I was an alien landing at the match from a far-off exoplanet.

I was new to the big-match party. At 26, I had a clutch of Candidates appearances on my CV and no inkling of what a beast a match for the World Championship title could be. Kasparov, by contrast, had set the benchmark for thoroughness in theoretical preparation, was steeped in chess history and, having grown up in the Soviet Union hanging around legends like Mikhail Botvinnik and Boris Spassky, had the kind of perspective on such encounters that I obviously lacked. He was already a five-time World Champion and ranked No. 1 in the world; I may have been placed second, but to his wealth of match experience mine pretty much hovered around zilch.

Undoubtedly, he was the overwhelming favourite by a distance and I expected him to come at me, so I focused my energies on not going down Short's path and losing too many games at the start, because when early losses strike, the score becomes hopeless with no chance of a turnaround and the result is a given. (In 1993, Short had lost three of the first four games and Kasparov had taken the title with a massive 12.5–7.5 score.) I knew my match against Kasparov was going to be a protracted battle, so the idea was not to push anything early.

I had a feeling Kasparov took me fairly seriously for the match – possibly because he couldn't read me fully and couldn't tell for himself when I was playing safe. Also, one of his greatest fears then was losing his title to complacency. Kasparov was by nature supremely confident, but not the kind who's lulled into overconfidence, and he was hardly so for the match against me. His score against me, starting out at a negative in 1991, had pushed him into a position of advantage with wins in Dortmund in 1992, Linares in both 1993 and 1994, and at the Tal Memorial the following year.

For me, the match against Kasparov turned out to be a listicle of all the things I shouldn't attempt in scenarios of similar magnitude. Before the match, I had done everything by myself – negotiating with seconds, booking flights and hotels, and inviting close friends to come over and provide moral support. I presumed it would simply be an extension of moving into a house of my own a year ago, in Collado Mediano, a kilometre away from Nieves and Maurice's home. Having friends around, I had surmised, would help reduce the pressure. For the high-strung tense encounter it turned out to be, this was, in retrospect, a hare-brained idea. My parents landed in New York ahead of the match and when my father realized I didn't even have a match contract worked out, he took on the job of negotiating one with the PCA. Of course, the PCA had trained lawyers on their side and my father had neither much experience in such matters nor great insight into the workings of the chess world. Yet, his initiative of having the terms laid down on paper was a prudent one that could come to my aid in the instance of any eventuality or breach.

Just before the match began, I ran into a piece of news that surprised me and caused me a brief flicker of pain: Kramnik, I heard, was part of Kasparov's team. I had met Kramnik for the first time during a tournament in Moscow in 1989, an incredibly tall boy, roughly six years younger than me, in shorts and a T-shirt, sporting a mullet, with a lit cigarette held gingerly between his fingers. I parked him at the back of my mind while I got busy with my Candidates appearances. He returned to the forefront quite suddenly after the Dortmund tournament in 1992, which he won. There was a lot of chatter, with everyone raving about him, and Kasparov commented then that Kramnik was the greatest talent ever seen and was likely to be his next challenger.

Soon Kramnik and I began playing each other regularly at tournaments and forged a harmless rivalry, since both of us understood that we weren't yet direct threats to each other. He was warm, friendly and affectionate, with a wry sense of humour, and often made the most startling statements with acute nonchalance. I'd always believed that we were fellow rivals when it came to playing Kasparov, and it had never occurred to me that he would choose to work in a team against me. I collected myself soon enough as I realized I probably didn't have the right to feel offended and moved on.

It seems funny to think now that the city that features in one of my favourite songs, performed by Frank Sinatra, offered me both a match venue and the learning of a lifetime.

Kasparov and I were to play 20 games over five weeks – four each week without adjournments or additional rest days, and on a time control of two hours for 40 moves in each game, one hour for the next 20 moves, followed by 30 minutes for the remainder. Manhattan looked startlingly breathtaking from 1,310 feet in the sky and spectators paid five times the regular observation deck fee of $15 to be seated in the viewing area of the match. The glass walls that separated us from them and the rest of the world weren't soundproofed well enough and we could hear the chatter and footsteps of antsy visitors, and also, on occasion, commentators Maurice Ashley and Daniel King's narration of our moving pieces.

We began with eight draws, a record number for a World Championship then. When badgered at the post-game press conference over it, I offered a slightly cocky 'it's not rock and roll' comment, to the delight of the journalists present. I was the first to land a punch and break free from the deadlock with a win in the ninth game for a 5–4 lead, and joked to arbiter Carol Jarecki that 'I'd pulled a tiger's whisker'. Kasparov had unsurprisingly chosen the Najdorf Sicilian (usually Black's answer to 1.e4, with a pawn setting up camp in the d4 square and denying White a central target) for the fifth time in nine games. I threw in a rook sacrifice for a knight; he furrowed his brow, thought for eight whole minutes and then accepted the offer. My White pawns swarmed down the middle, his attempts at mounting an attack spectacularly collapsed, and he resigned on move 35.

Kasparov returned an ill-tempered, marauding highwayman in the tenth game. He banged his pieces on the board, leapt out of his chair after making his moves, and occasionally walked out of the room, slamming the door behind him. It was presumably an effort to rattle me and I found it thoroughly unpleasant.

In both games 10 and 11, I lost the battle in the opening itself. I had reason to regret not using my Centre Counter in game 10 despite knowing that Kasparov had been trying to break my Open Spanish for a while. To repeat it then (after having employed it earlier in game 6) just felt naive. On move 15, Kasparov planted his knight on b3 and I went on to devour 45 minutes of the total 120 minutes stipulated for the first 40 moves, leaving 25 more moves to be played in the remaining time. The charge of the White pawns and an imminent mate had me resign in 38 moves. My fatal error lay in being predictable and repeating the variation for which Kasparov had already found a workaround. I'd slipped into autopilot mode and a reverie that had me believing that things would take care of themselves.

This led me into a situation I was thoroughly unprepared for. In game 11, Kasparov uncorked the Dragon variation of the Sicilian Defence, a feared counterattack to White's 1.e4 push and a line he had never employed before in a major match. I responded with the Yugoslav attack, a double-edged sword, which has White castling on the queenside and Black castling on the kingside, throwing open a sharp, gnarly option for attacking each other's king. Kasparov extended a draw offer on move 19, which I turned down and foolishly threw open my position while attempting to win a rook for my knight. I went on to fall behind him by a full point (6–5) in the match. It soon dawned on me that the blows that had struck Short two years ago were now raining down on me thick and fast. The feeling of going to the board suddenly not being able to recognize myself, playing abysmally, losing and returning, swept over me. This continued for a few days. I had control over nothing. It felt like I was swimming around without a single surface to touch.

Our fortunes swung wildly in game 14. I played a Center Counter, went on to decline a draw offer and managed to have him keel over into a complex middle game with a knight push on e5. From a relatively inferior position, Kasparov mounted an assault with a knight on g4 and e5, and a pawn on a6, and I could sense that he was relishing the tension, like a man watching a snowstorm from the warmth of his fireplace. I ran into time trouble and lost, and Kasparov wrapped up the championship 10.5–7.5 four games later.

A couple of weeks after the match, I ran into Kramnik in Paris, near the Champs-Élysées. He threw his shoulders up and made an awkward gesture, almost as if to say he didn't mean to team up against me but that it was more an opportunity to work with a mind like Kasparov's that he didn't want to miss. We exchanged smiles and decided to let the matter pass.

Frankly, I was not ready for a match of that magnitude. At the time, computers were nowhere close to performing the way they do now and the match taught me how much I had left to learn. Looking back, I'd say the volume of preparation I did through the match is perhaps what I do now in a day's time.

Contrasting that with the World Championship match I played against Carlsen in 2013, it's easy to see how substantially the value of experience has diminished because of the way computers have evolved.

♛

In June 1996, I got married to Aruna. Our parents had picked us out for each other in what was a conventional arranged marriage match, or, as Frederic puts it, a 'catalogue wedding'. We barely knew each other, but since we found no reason to say 'no' we said 'yes'. Aruna often compares my decision to marry her with the way I used to play then – fast, and not with a whole lot of thought put in before I made the decisive move. We spoke over pre-booked international calls while I was travelling for tournaments. She was usually surrounded by her entire family as she spoke to me, being goaded into making polite queries about food and the weather wherever I was. Neither of us knew what to tell the other, so a typical conversation would progress somewhat like: 'How are you?' 'I'm fine, how's the weather?' 'It's cold here, what about there?' 'Oh, here it's hot.' 'Okay, bye.'

Nieves and Maurice flew to Madras to attend our wedding. One evening, in typical dad avatar, my father dropped a provocative taunt that alluded to my sheltered existence courtesy my mother through the early years of my life, and later Nieves and Maurice. 'I'm willing to lay a bet. Vishy will never be a World Champion,' he declared. On his part, the statement appeared to have been made more in the way of creating shock value than with any real intent, but Nieves roundly took offence. It didn't really affect me since I knew my father and his pet peeves, his love for a good rant and his need to do some tough talking with his kids once in a while. I accepted it as something I could laugh over later rather than take literally; Nieves, however, agreed to lay a punt. I wasn't privy to the details that were agreed upon, but Nieves had taken my father's remark as an affront to her unwavering belief in my prospects of becoming a World Champion and would have willingly thrown in anything.

Contrary to the jokes in the circuit about me losing a whole bunch of Elo points after my marriage, I had a phenomenal result in Dortmund in July that year. I tied for first place with Kramnik, having scored a full point over the rest of the eight-player field. The following year, 1997, was even better for me with a symphony of uninterrupted sparkling results. I won the Amber Tournament and the Credit Suisse Classic in Biel, was joint first at the Category XXIX annual Dos Hermanas tournament in Spain and the Invesbanka tournament in Belgrade and finished in second place at the Dortmund Sparkassen.

The baton of handling everything in my life, apart from chess, soon passed on from Nieves to Aruna. It evolved slowly, starting with Aruna offering to answer match-related emails or asking me to request organizers to write to her so she could manage the logistics of an upcoming tournament. Slight problems arose when she started to pack my suitcases for tournaments. From living alone to suddenly having to explain to others how you like things done feels like an imposition, especially when you don't fully appreciate that other people may have different but better ways of doing things. From tossing soiled clothes into my suitcase, I suddenly had fresh laundry neatly arranged in it before I travelled, alongside colour-coordinated socks and woollens to weather the Arctic cold or welcome the Mediterranean spring. Medicines for every ailment with a name, though thankfully just short of an oxygen cylinder, were packed in too.

I also eventually had to give up on the strange fetish I had for multiple phone plans, sorting them according to which worked better at what time of the day, depending on which part of the world I was making a call to. My marriage was very nearly on the rocks in the initial months since every time Aruna wanted to call her parents in Madras from Madrid or wherever we were travelling to for tournaments, I'd inundate her with complex details of the most effective plan to use. It irritated her no end and she soon made sure I threw that habit out of the window.

The next phase was that of letting go of the need to control every detail to do with my tournaments and travel.

In a year or two, this turned into a massive relief for me. Packing suitcases was a harmless chore, with no emotional baggage attached to it, but I found negotiating contracts, booking hotels and flight tickets, checking with seconds on their availability and waiting for them to reply to be a whole lot of unnecessary stress. The improvement in my results between the match against Kasparov in 1995 and the Candidates tournament I played in Groningen, the Netherlands, in December 1997, I believe, came simply from me not having to handle everyday matters and being able to concentrate solely on my preparation.

Of course, I had other demons to battle, namely the brazen bias and politicking in the chess world.

FIDE's system of knockout matches had replaced the Candidates tournament as the qualifier for the World Championship in 1995, but in the 1997–98 cycle, Karpov had been directly seeded into the final. So it came about that whoever won the knockout tournament in Groningen would qualify to play Karpov within a space of three days in the final to be held in Lausanne in January 1998.

It was a grossly unfair deal, but I told myself that since I'd decided to play, I'd put these thoughts aside and concentrate on the game. I managed this well for as long as I was in Groningen. It helped to have the tournament divided into two parts and the games played at different venues. Since Karpov wasn't at Groningen we didn't have to brood over how prejudiced the conditions of the championship were every day that we were there. Kasparov was dismissive of the knockout format to determine a challenger and refused to be a part of it and Kramnik too pulled out over the unfair privileges being extended to Karpov.

Once the tournament commenced, in the first match, I beat Predrag Nikolić effortlessly, came agonizingly close to losing to Alexander Khalifman in the second round, but survived. That's the funny thing about knockouts. It's almost like being able to see the car crash you're going to be a victim of in the next instant and not knowing how to stop it. All I could think of during that lost position at the board against Khalifman was, 'My goodness, if I lose this we'll have to pack our bags and leave this evening.' Then, almost as though there had been some sort of divine intervention, I found Khalifman aimlessly swatting about not knowing what to do, before he froze and agreed to a draw from what to me looked like a winning position. It's the kind of inexplicable miracle you can only be thankful for. I beat him in the tie-break thereafter and came out of the match feeling like I'd survived death itself. That deliverance lifted my spirits immensely and I played the rest of the tournament with a completely different zest. I won the rounds that followed – against Zoltán Almási, Alexei Shirov and Gelfand – without a spill into a tie-break. It was impressive, given that the prize money at stake was doubling with every round and if you survived till the third or fourth rounds you made as much money as you would in a whole year. Naturally, the players were all transfixed by both the money on offer and the prospect of playing for the title of World Champion.

In the final round, I faced Adams, whom I was better against in most of the four games we had played. Both of us were fatigued to the bone by then, since we'd spent pretty much the whole of December playing the tournament. For the final match, oddly enough, we hitched a ride together to the venue, since it was Christmas season and cabs were few. During the match, Adams was tenacious and the momentum oscillated until I finally won the ninth tie-break game to qualify for the match against Karpov. Suddenly, the unfairness of that match, something I'd been trying to push out of my mind, was looking me straight in the eye.

We hadn't planned our travel to Lausanne in advance since the outcome of the Candidates tournament couldn't have been foreseen, and we now realized, late in the day, that FIDE too had made no arrangements for the Groningen winner to reach Lausanne from Amsterdam and play Karpov in three days' time.

The flagrant unreasonableness of the whole scenario stung. But it's not a card you can play at a match you've agreed to be part of already. All you'll get for your carping is a few minutes of token sympathy. If you continue, by the second day people will look away, by the third everyone else will move on and by the fourth you're likely to be called a crank.

It was New Year's Eve and flights were overbooked. 'Once you get to Lausanne, we will take care of pretty much everything,' a FIDE official tried to placate us when confronted. Aruna smiled and replied that if we could get to Lausanne in the first place, we could take care of the rest ourselves. We somehow managed to get ourselves on a plane and landed in Lausanne, only to learn that FIDE had booked all its officials into hotel rooms but had made no provision whatsoever to accommodate the winner of the 21-day-long knockout tournament that was a qualifier for the final. Once again, we were left to wage a logistics battle on our own, with an impending match on our heads.

I had reached out to Yusupov and Leko, who were then in Hungary and Germany respectively, through a pay phone at Amsterdam's Schiphol Airport, and they both joined us at short notice. Ubilava had been with me through the tournament in Groningen and now, with the title match against Karpov ahead, the team needed to be expanded to prepare for one-on-one combat.

As the match proceeded, at the end of five games, Karpov opened up a one-point lead. I unleashed the Trompowsky, an aggressive queen's pawn opening, in the sixth and final game and managed to equalize scores to 3–3 and force a tie-break of two rapid games. I ended up losing both. It was almost as if I had been asked to run a 100-metre sprint after completing a cross-country marathon – and Karpov became the new World Champion.

The defeat rankled like few had before because I'd played the match against a loaded dice, come close to a win and then squandered it.

♛

It was in Wijk aan Zee, soon after my loss, that Karpov spoke of my inability to win a World Championship title while still justifying his own credentials despite the brazenly undue advantage he had received. He had been fresh, well rested and pottering around while I was almost 'brought in a coffin' to play him. When I heard his words that morning, the first thought that struck me was, 'Yes, I obviously don't have the strength of character to lie on a pool chair while my buddies at FIDE get me seeded into the final.' I was already working myself up to display my potential, and this swipe only reinforced the conviction I already had deep within – that nothing else mattered any more, I just had to win a title now. I had done all the admirable things short of winning, but I was acutely aware that my efforts wouldn't speak for me if I couldn't finish the job.

Suggestions of visiting a psychologist who could plug gaps, if any, in going from 'great player' to 'champion' popped up. Soon after Lausanne, on Aruna's insistence, we visited a sports psychologist for a single session. I didn't take to the idea too well as I simply didn't see myself confiding in a stranger for therapeutic purposes, so we dropped it soon after.

Sometimes, a rival's or a peer's success can offer an unlikely, unconscious spur. I had found Kramnik's win over Kasparov in the 2000 World Championship in London impressive and inspirational, mainly for the way he had managed to make Kasparov seem helpless. It's not an easy thing to do – hardly anyone had managed it before. Unlike me, Kramnik didn't make the mistake of being predictable against Kasparov. His Berlin Defence looked invincible but in game 9 he switched openings and switched back again in game 11. I thought that was pure genius. The deft approach he showed in stepping slightly aside was brilliant. He couldn't entirely be faulted for coming off as slightly supercilious after his win, suggesting that while working for Kasparov against me, he didn't find a shred of evidence in my game that suggested I had a strategy worked out. He observed that I had presumed I could just turn up, do what

I always did and expect to win. He may not have meant any malice, but somehow his words stayed with me.

When I reflected on them, I felt it was perhaps true that I had lacked the intent and the mental fortitude to win a World Championship title. For a long time in my career, I wasn't quite fired up by the ambition to become a World Champion. Ubilava had occasionally tried to spark a longing in me to reach beyond the distinctions of being the 'first Indian' or 'first Asian' in various categories, but I was content travelling to tournaments around the world, playing good games, putting up a decent fight and being known as a strong player. It was my match against Kasparov in New York in 1995 that changed my attitude.

To be the first to break the deadlock of eight draws between us with a win, and then go on to implode was a lesson for me on how everything could go awry if I remained too predictable a player. I had thrown myself under the bus by making the obvious rookie mistake of not switching openings and turning into a sitting duck. The way the match went distilled every aspect of what I had been lacking and flashed it on to a projection screen before me. It drove me to base my preparations for future matches on all that I hadn't explored during the 1995 match – primarily the ability to switch, surprise and stay unaffected by psychological duress. It also became evident to me that the transition from being a strong player to becoming a champion wasn't going to happen on its own. I had to want it ardently enough.

Five years since that time in New York, after I'd weathered enough near-misses, including the one against Karpov in

Lausanne, it was time to collect my dues. When the first leg of the FIDE World Championship tournament in 2000 took place in New Delhi, with the Indian infotech company NIIT hopping on board as a sponsor, I already knew deep within that this was my chance.

The knockout tournament consisted of two-game matches, followed by tie-breaks at faster time controls in the instance of a draw. The only blip I suffered in what was otherwise smooth sailing was in the quarter-finals, yet again against Khalifman. I ended up playing four tie-break games in a row on my birthday (11 December), and I slithered out of tricky positions in both, with a particularly close shave in the second. Topalov, who was in the audience, was to remark after the win, 'Gosh, Vishy should be called the snake [not the tiger] of Madras!'

That salvage gave me a fresh boost of confidence and I was certain that Khalifman would be raging at himself for having missed on a chance to eliminate me. When Aruna, Ubilava and I met backstage, relief was writ large on our faces and we knew the worst was over. I went on to beat Khalifman in the fifth game following four successive draws to move into the semi-finals against Adams, and wrapped up the match.

We landed in Tehran, where the final was to be held, feeling woozy with upset stomachs, but with every instinct telling us that the title was mine for the taking. Both Ubilava and I were dead on our feet from the long, unending stretch of games, and I wished Pablo San Segundo Carrillo, a dear friend who'd help me with training ahead of the New Delhi match but wasn't travelling with us, could join the team in

Iran's capital city. To my surprise – and immense relief – Aruna had already made the arrangements and Pablo arrived in Tehran an hour after us. He was the kind of happy spirit who could lighten up long training sessions and we teased him by giving him the title of 'Señor Corte Inglés' (alluding to Spain's largest department and fashion store chain) for his sharp suits and fine sweaters.

Before the match, a Spanish ambassador who'd arrived to offer support to his compatriot Shirov, who was to play me in the six-game final, leant towards him, pumped his fists and in a fairly audible tone grunted, *'Da le bien*. Give him good.' He had no idea, of course, that I, seated right next to Shirov, spoke Spanish and caught the pep talk. Shirov, who had Latvian roots, was flush with embarrassment, and explained to the ambassador that I lived in Spain and was more familiar with Spanish culture and the language than he was, though he had a Spanish passport. The ambassador turned scarlet and awkward, but we later made up over some good-hearted banter.

Shirov wasn't supposed to be an easy opponent. He was in blazing form; he had beaten me at both the Linares and the Amber tournaments in March that year and had only two years ago, in 1998, got the better of Kramnik in a 10-game match held to pick Kasparov's challenger. Eventually, the funding for the match had fallen through and he never got to play against Kasparov. In Tehran, though, Shirov's game turned out to be a pale shadow of his rousing past performances. My Delhi belly was to be the fullest extent of trouble I had to face in the final and I didn't run into any real problems at the board. After a drawn first game, I won the next three to take the title. At last, I was a World Champion.

When I called Nieves to break the news of my win, she gurgled with laughter, congratulated me in a hurry and then whipped out the wager she'd been holding on to for four years. 'Tell your dad I want my money,' she said.

Viswanathan Anand v. Garry Kasparov (1-0)
(White) (Black)

Game 9, 1995 PCA World Championship, New York
WHITE WINS

At this stage in the game, I played rook to d5, confident that it could not be taken because my pawns would be robust. I didn't really see a way forward if Kasparov didn't take it. Had he waited and not taken the rook, my advantage would have been very small. Thankfully, he took it and in a few moves I was well on my way to my only win in the match.

♛

The match against Kasparov in New York in 1995 changed my attitude from being content playing good games and winning occasionally to being completely driven to becoming the World Champion. In the years that followed, I realized how that single match had distilled every aspect of what I lacked – the ability to be flexible, unpredictable and stay unaffected by psychological duress. It also became evident to me that the transition from being a strong player to becoming a champion wasn't going to happen on its own. I had to want it ardently enough. Doing everything admirably well matters very little if you can't finish the job.

SEVEN

THE GIFT
AND THE GRIT

MAKING TALENT WORK HARD

AT BEST, I WAS AN ODDITY ON THE WORLD CHESS SCENE. A NON-Soviet (and a non-Westerner) from a land that sounded unfamiliar, exotic and far-flung from the rumblings of the sport. Phonetically too my name was a misfit among the Soviet cluster of chess players' names that rhymed with each other's and almost sounded familial.

For the Soviets, chess was a national obsession. Powerful state sponsorship motored the monolithic chess machine and everywhere you looked – parks, trains, smoke-filled club corners – you'd spot both old and young faces furrowed in quiet reflection, thumping pieces on the table or straddling a board on their knees. Brides added chessboards to their wedding trousseaus and when you travelled you got the feeling that every cab driver in the country could checkmate you with a smirk. Additionally, one got the impression that the state didn't take too kindly to its subjects' camaraderie with non-Soviets. During those years, Soviet players may even have been shadowed by the state's secret service agency, the KGB, when they joined foreigners like me for an innocent walk in Moscow.

By 1990, around the time I broke into the upper reaches of the sport, Perestroika had already been around for five years and the dissolution of the Union was near. The wave of reformative ideas sweeping the country effected a change in perspective among Soviet players – they began to look out for themselves and shed the sense of being a collective, singular unit. The rivalries among them were intense and quite a few of their players rooted for me against fellow Soviets whom they disliked. I recall those as my innocent years. I was 21 years old, wide-eyed and disbelieving, living a dream.

Somewhere between the endless blitz sessions at the Tal Chess Club in Madras, winning the title of World Junior Champion and achieving the distinction of becoming a Grandmaster, 'talent' had appended itself to my name. In 1991, I banished that postfix with wins over Soviet luminaries Kasparov, Karpov, Kamsky and Korchnoi at the Interpolis International Tournament in Tilburg, in the Netherlands, to finish third. That year, I also became the first Asian to make the FIDE World Championship quarter-finals after beating Dreev in Madras. Yet, it was the title that I plucked at the category-18 Reggio Emilia Super Grandmaster tournament in 1991–92 in northern Italy – featuring nine other top players, all of them Soviet citizens – that turned out to be the definitive point of inflection. I finished ahead of both Karpov and Kasparov. By the time the tournament ended, the Soviet Union had dissolved and the joke of me being the last Soviet-era chess champion wrote itself out.

It's at this point that I discovered that 'talent' is a word people use to describe you when they want to express good-hearted empathy. It merely reflects that you're not yet a threat to their dominance or their prize fund flow. It's when they trash-talk you – like they did after my surprise coup in Italy – that you know you're respected, maybe even feared.

Whether talent makes hard work redundant or hard work makes talent irrelevant is to me an unfair argument. The compelling need to pit hard work against talent or claim the dispensability of either is unnecessary. The way I see it, talent is a lot like a plant. When it's watered with hard work, it grows, branches out and blooms. Deprived of nourishment, the plant simply withers away. With hard work, talent gains in depth and scope, and uncovers abilities that were earlier unexplored. Talent and hard work, therefore, aren't conflicting forces orbiting in separate galaxies; they are complementary to each other and provide one another with sustenance.

I hate to undermine the worth of talent. Unquestionably, talent exists. It's no myth or hokum. Your talent tells you that you're cut out for something. It points you towards what you can do effortlessly and what your potential career could be. However, talent isn't everything. Knowledge and growth don't come easily. You have to be willing to put in the hours and the effort, sometimes even without visible progress, because one day, unexpectedly, the results will flower. But without that work, it's unlikely to happen. Eventually, hard work is not just about plugging away at something.

It's thinking intelligently about what you want to achieve, the goals you're setting yourself, how you're improving and how you can incorporate all of this into the list of things that will help you scale that peak.

If you look at a sample group of precocious youth who have been exposed to a sport around the same time and have worked equally hard, there is no cogent explanation for the difference in their results other than the superior competence of a few in a certain domain or skill set, or what we call 'aptitude'. Talent makes itself seen – you can tell from the feverish pace at which some pick up a certain subject, while others take much longer to wrap their heads around it – before hard work takes over. Quite often, we come across two players who've spent their entire lives playing a sport and have risen through the ranks. For one of them success flows easily, almost effortlessly, while the other may have a more laboured progress. But when the latter hits a bend and begins to play well, I don't ascribe the turnaround to discipline alone – I believe they are actually tapping into a pre-existing resource. In general, though, a person who's working hard and doing all the right things will invariably pull ahead of someone who may be talented but is not putting in as much effort.

History posits the brilliance of Bobby Fischer as an example. Fischer learnt to play chess after his younger sister brought a chess set home from a candy store. By age 14, he won the US Championship, and a year later became the youngest Grandmaster in the world. Did he possess talent? Undoubtedly. He was obsessed with chess, and something about the game clicked in his head in a way that it didn't for anyone else. But can his success be ascribed to talent alone? I don't think so. He worked incredibly hard at driving his love for chess to achieve results. Fischer took time off from playing in competitions to study games of the nineteenth-century greats and to learn Russian, an ability he then employed to read innumerable Russian chess magazines and books. In the Soviet-run chess ecosystem of his time, mastering their tongue and teachings was a clever move indeed. It also spoke of Fischer's commitment to winning and the incredible effort he put into achieving what he did.

I suppose I should speak for myself here. Playing chess came naturally to me from a very young age and I had an aptitude for it. In fact, my 'aptitude' might explain why I was attracted to the game in the first place – it's when something intuitively makes sense to you and immediately grabs your attention; it comes at you leaping and lunging, and lodges itself in your mind. Growing up, I was fascinated by the genius of the mathematician Srinivasa Ramanujan. I received his biography, *The Man Who Knew Infinity*, as a gift and was enthralled by his story – this was a boy who, with no formal training in mathematics, strummed up analyses and conclusions his peers at hallowed foreign universities hadn't, and went on to have a profound and extraordinary impact on the subject. I recall reading about our common roots – both of us belong to the southern Indian state of Tamil Nadu (his family was from Kumbakonam and mine from Mayiladuthurai, then Mayavaram, less than 40 kilometres apart) – and how he would make notes on his observations in the dim light of a flickering lamp with no access to mathematics books. I somehow found his story relatable, possibly because I was largely self-taught in the sport I played, far removed from the fulcrum of chess learning, the Soviet Union.

Equally, there were many others who started out in the sport around the same time as I did, but drifted away and went on to find success in other fields. It could be that their aptitude in another domain sought them out. The prodigious Joshua Waitzkin, who took on chess hustlers as a seven-year-old in New York's Washington Square Park and won his first national championship at the age of nine, was thrown into the vortex of public expectation as a teen after a book on him written by his father was turned into a major motion picture. Later, he just couldn't stand the game any more. He faced a crisis out of a sense of alienation from a sport he loved deeply, and decided to leave it behind and search for something new. He started meditating, studying psychology and philosophy and, at 21, made what appeared to be a surprise – and eventually successful – shift from the scholastic chess scene in the US to the Chinese martial art form of Tai Chi Chuan. There are others too who are drawn to chess and achieve outstanding results, but perhaps out of overtraining and staleness burn out early.

While it was clear that I was gifted, I didn't have a serious breakthrough until the summer of 1983, the magic year when my results suddenly turned sunny side up. I was surrounded by players who worked equally hard on their game, but somehow my brain had strung it all together nicely and I went on to win two major open tournaments, dotted with higher-rated players, in Tamil Nadu, topped the Under 16 National Championship with a flawless 9/9 score and qualified for the Under 16 World Championship, all in the same year.

What remained a constant through this time was my ability to play fast. It came naturally to me and was nurtured and reinforced through my blitz-stacked years at the Tal Chess Club. For a characteristically deliberative sport, speed play can give a player the reputation of being rash and foolish. My father, who is usually regimental in his ways, however, encouraged me to be intuitive at the board and I found a quiet validation in his words, *'Unakku* fast *aadanam na ni aadu, baba.* If you want to play fast, play fast, son.' I earned the sobriquet 'Lightning Kid' while still a teen with a cap pulled over my face. (I started wearing it more out of compulsion than as a fashion choice. A player from Thane, Arun Vaidya, whom I ran into at national tournaments, had a nagging habit of swinging his keychain around his index finger and I began wearing a cap to shut out the jangling distraction.)

It wasn't solely about making quick moves. An old friend from my junior days, the Canadian-Russian player Evgeny Bareev noticed that I possessed a unique gift – I could see more on the board than most players did within the first minute. Alongside, though, he observed that I seemed to have great difficulty in building on my initial impressions, or going deep and uncovering hidden resources in a position. It's as if my brain simply switched off at some point. It was a weak spot I had to work on to fix. It wasn't just a question of telling myself that I had to think longer before I made a move; I knew I had to train thoroughly in negotiating certain positions to find a way to go deeper. Throughout my career, my trainers have told me to think more over certain positions and, at the board, look for the ones in which I could allow my natural talent to take over. Following their advice, I've found that studying examples of the resources I had previously missed is the most effective method I can use to find the positions that are most advantageous to me during a game.

Essentially, there are two kinds of chess players – the ones who belong to the Soviet school of the game, who're given to methodical learning, exposed systematically to the basic principles and heuristics, and the second group which comprises players drawn from countries without a serious tradition in the sport, who are unstructured in their learning, spend endless hours playing blitz and improvise at the board. The two styles, however, don't remain disparate for life and eventually converge. Those like me, who belong to the second category and have come through free learning systems, learn how to study seriously and pick up on opening preparations later, though we never entirely compensate for missing out on the other kind of training while growing up. On the other hand, those who approach chess systematically often have to learn to be comfortable in chaos and accept that not everything at the board can be solved in a regular way, and that in order to be successful they have to acquire spontaneity, intuitiveness and imbibe the ability to take calculated risks. Since I belonged to the second group, the Soviets initially dismissed me as an upstart, a 'coffee-house player' – a pejorative description for someone who's not serious or professional about the game, experiments a lot and generally isn't up to scratch.

It's not that I've not had to live with the failings of my style of playing on occasion – the torment of games where I didn't pull my hand back in time or allowed myself an extra minute of thought and walked right into a waiting trap has been quite acute. Truthfully, though, my blitz-playing years were more a boon than a handicap. The absence of serious, formal training lent flexibility to my style and I wasn't capsized by problems, no matter how unusual or far from the regular patterns they were.

I've also seen both kinds of talented players – those who work on their talent and those who kick off their flip-flops and hope to be rewarded for simply possessing a gift. There are players across different sports who are marked out early as being talented, but who don't progress far over the years. It's perhaps because they haven't built on their innate abilities or what was initially on display was, in fact, the fullest extent of their limited talent. I've been through stretches in my career when I too have thought I'll coast along because things seemed to come easier to me. But that kind of attitude had its consequences, and I am, as a result, a committed subscriber to the principles of hard work.

From my early years I developed the habit of reading tournament journals filled with game descriptions. I was perhaps naive and it never occurred to me that I should question the methods detailed in them or be led by my own value judgements. Since I was open to fresh ideas and not sanctimonious about the ones I practised, I could cull bits of novelties from the games I read about and try to fit them into my preparatory work.

Talent and hard work apart, you also need luck for things to come together at the right time. I have had that on several occasions when I needed it the most. Had I not qualified for the Candidates tournament in 1993 my career could have taken a different turn and shape. As I see it, in my case, it was not enough to be talented. I had to put in a lot of hard work, and I also got the breaks I needed – World Junior Champion (1987), Grandmaster (1988) and qualifying for the World Championship cycle (1993) – at the most fitting junctures.

Two years later, winning the Candidates tournament against Kamsky in Las Palmas on the Canary Islands in March 1995 opened up the path for my first crack at the title of World Champion against Kasparov. I buried myself in preparations through January and February, ahead of the Candidates, with my trainers, Yusupov and Ubilava, at home in Spain. I went for a run every morning in the mountains and since my mother had come over, we left for Las Palmas together.

I lost the first game on time. Essentially, I just sat there motionless while my clock ran down. It seemed like a complete catastrophe to be known as among the fastest players in the world and yet lose on this factor. In fact, my inaction in that first game raised suspicions that the water I had been served was spiked and Nieves stepped in to insist that in all subsequent games only the water we carried was to be given to me to drink. I can't really say I shrugged off that loss or that I took it in my stride, but I did show up for business the next day and managed an easy draw with

Black. I beat Kamsky in the third game, which calmed me down and reassured me that the first game had been an aberration. We then landed in a rut of five draws before what came to be a fantastic result for me in game 9. My move, 26.Nd1 – where my knight rerouted its path, stubbed Black's threats (with its knight on g5), had my queen guarding the square and stalled the knights' exchange – turned out to be a brilliant manoeuvre.

No matter how many unforgettable games you play, eventually, everyone hits a wall. You realize that people whom you'd beaten easily are suddenly pulling ahead. Lying on your back and waiting for a marvel doesn't seem like the best idea any more, so you scramble to your feet, work hard and race ahead to catch up.

I've run into a wall many times in my career when I've needed to take a break, pause and find my way back, but I've never been sufficiently disenchanted to leave chess or search for something more appealing. Maybe, if I had to toil longer for a Grandmaster title, perhaps a couple of years more than I did, then I would have looked back at things differently. The Grandmaster distinction, since it was rare then, opened many doors for me, including the ability to compete in top-level tournaments and play against the world's best players. For today's players, it's unlikely to offer a major bonus and might kick open fewer doors. Whenever I've felt satiated and sick of chess, my natural response has been to switch off and leave the game alone for a while, but my love for the game has never soured enough for me to walk away.

Success rubrics may not put this together well enough –

yes, talent is undeniable, but so are the unexpected breaks, the signposts that tell you that you stand a shot at your dream. It's here that hard work pops up and waves at you. The harder you work, the greater the chances of getting these breaks. Without them, it's easy to fall out of love with your passion and disown your talent.

Viswanathan Anand v. Gata Kamsky (1–0)
(White)　　　　　　　　(Black)

Game 9, 1995 Candidates Tournament, Las Palmas
WHITE WINS

The match was tied at this stage. But all the years of studying the Ruy Lopez paid off now. My move, the 26.Nd1, effectively stalled Ng5 and prepared Nc3 to be unleashed on the weak, unaided b5 pawn. This is one of the most creative games I have played.

♛

The way I see it, talent is a lot like a plant. When it's watered with hard work, it grows and blooms. Deprived of nourishment, the plant simply withers away. With hard work, talent gains in depth and scope, and uncovers newer abilities that were earlier unexplored. And hard work is not just about plugging away at something. It involves thinking intelligently about what you want to achieve, the goals you're setting, how you're improving on your innate skills or talents, and how you can incorporate all of this into the list of things that will help you scale that peak.

EIGHT

MINING THE MIND AND MACHINES

DECISION-MAKING, DATA AND A NEW GIANT ON THE BLOCK

TRULY, I WAS IN A FIX. ON THE BOARD BEFORE ME, WAITING TO be unlocked, lay the variation over which I'd put myself and the team through the grind during my World Championship match against Gelfand a year ago. It hadn't come into use then, but here it was now, ready to be played in the fourth round of the Wijk aan Zee tournament, 2013. The problem was I couldn't remember anything about the work we'd done a year ago except one niggling detail.

I imagined my trainer, Nielsen, scowling in a corner of the hall. It was the last tournament in which Nielsen would be working with me, after having been a part of my team and indeed my family for close to a decade. He was to join Carlsen's team shortly. Despite that, when I proposed the idea of working together for a final time for the Wijk aan Zee tournament, he had happily agreed. The understanding between us was that if Carlsen qualified for the World

Championship against me that year, Nielsen would stay neutral and step away from any preparatory work for or against me.

Aronian, the defending champion of the annual competition, sat across me, listening to me breathe, waiting for my hand to push a piece. I had two choices: To back down and move somewhere else on the board, or press down the main line, trying to trace out the sketchy notes from a forgotten training session. Although I couldn't draw up the exact positions I'd worked on, I knew that sticking to the main line was good for Black.

It was like knowing about a treasure hidden in a forest and setting out to look for it with just a few snippets of information available – such as that it's under a tree with three fruits hanging from its branches and the tree itself is not far from a waterbody. There could be two trees that meet the description, but after considering all the information available you have to refine your decision and make the best guess you can. Without those bits of information, the forest is like any other forest, and you wouldn't want to waste your time poking around in it. Similarly, in chess, in a scenario where you don't know if there's something useful buried in a position, prudence would suggest that you simply stick to what you know.

At the board, I initially felt lost. The information I had from my team and our past work on the position was that the main line was good for Black, and yet it seemed contradictory to what I saw before me now. All I could remember was one little nuance – that my knight had eventually got to d3. Nothing else. I sat there, my brain turning into mulch, my mind screaming that there must be a better way and trying to work out the line.

The parallels between the game that had me flummoxed and a classic game that I had read about as a child – played in Łódž, Poland, between Gersz Rotlewi and Akiba Rubinstein – were manifest. It was the same knight whipping up the attack and the White king was being browbeaten by the bishop duo on the exact diagonals. With no other cues to hang on to, I looked hard at the board, drilling deeper and deeper into my mind, going over the line again and again to make sure the positions matched the one thing I remembered, while I tried to mentally stencil out a plausible line before setting off on my wild scavenger hunt.

I remember thinking at one stage how worried Nielsen must be. Some part of him may have been shocked at my amnesiac behaviour at the board, while the other wondered what I was getting at. At the end of my prolonged musing – over a whole 30 minutes – the bishop sacrifice I offered up to gain the diagonal with Bc5 wiped the colour off Aronian's face. I then abandoned my knight, offering it up to be taken by a pawn with Nde5. It cleared the path for my queen and Aronian went on to walk right into a mate. Every player goes on to create that one thing of absolute, peerless beauty. This one was mine; one of the finest games of my life. I'd managed to piece together the half-memory of a classic game, my own preparatory data in the area and trusted my intuition to stay persistent in the hope of crawling to the other end of the tunnel where I'd find light and vindication.

One of the trickiest questions in chess is how many moves one has to think ahead. This is different from the number of moves you *ought* to think ahead. It is a question you have to solve every day and in every game. The Danish Grandmaster Bent Larsen once famously said, 'All long variations are wrong variations,' while the legendary World Champion José Raúl Capablanca, when asked how many moves ahead he looked while playing, responded with the humblebrag, 'Only one, but it's the right one!' The basic answer is that if the path ahead is like a highway and you simply have to follow it, then it's possible to see far ahead since it's a straight road before you. The alternative is entering a dense thicket, where after every step there is a choice of three or four steps, and you have to evaluate which one you are going to choose – and that's not all. For each step you take, your opponent has three or four responses, which you will again have to counter individually. In these kinds of positions, you invariably see less. In fact, the longer the calculations, the higher the chances of making a mistake.

In my mind, you need to calculate the choices and resources at hand to navigate the situation you're in, but you should also be armed with a wider perspective in case a new problem arises at the end of a long line. Also, if you've gone too far into a variation and are faced with a block, you should have the ability to return and second-guess the stage at which you may have missed something, and try to arrive at a balance between choosing what is feasible and gambling on a long variation in finding your way out.

Players also often wade into a time-related problem, instances where they have too little time to play the required move, because they are being indecisive and don't trust their calculations enough. My problem is slightly different: My intuition tends to behave like a child who gives an answer and immediately wants to know if it is correct. When I feel I know the answer to the problem staring me in the face, I make my move, not exactly because I'm dying of curiosity to know the outcome but just to be certain that it's right. In response, if my opponent spends a lot of time pondering over my move and considering his options, it annoys me no end.

The game against Karjakin, which won me the Candidates title and a rematch against Carlsen in 2014 was one such example. Aronian, who had been snapping at my heels until then, had just lost a game, and Karjakin perhaps thought he'd try to press a drawn position for as long as he could, essentially to take a shot at getting me to crack and throw my game away. He was perhaps trying to trick me into believing he had trouble in store for me, just to see how far I'd go. The only way I would get a good night's sleep, I knew, was if I sat tight and saw myself through, instead of drifting off impatiently and giving in to his ploy. I did indeed go all the way. At the end of the game, once we finally agreed on a draw, I joked to Karjakin how badly I'd wanted to murder him a few minutes ago for putting me through such awful agony.

A problem I face often, and one that still invokes a certain degree of surprise, is playing my move and then realizing that I had the wrong answer in the first place. In theory, when I have an hour on the clock, all I need to do is think for a little longer – the easiest thing to do really. But sometimes I'm so wound up that I can't see things clearly and I make a move without fully thinking it through. Imposing on yourself the need to take time and think before making a move is a helpful habit to have. Not giving in to provocation is another cue. Quite often, I find myself biting the bait, like I did at the 2017 London Chess Classic against Ian Nepomniachtchi. I knew I had a solid line, but I got caught in a fit of wanting to challenge him and call his bluff. Thinking that I'd figure it out somehow, I ended up wandering down a line for which I had zero preparation, and I lost the game horribly.

The essence of chess is identifying which approach works best against an opponent because what people hate doing is what they'll eventually do badly.

While I have used this against my opponents time and again, it's been used effectively against me just as often. When I was younger, I wasn't up to pace with Kasparov or Kramnik in the aspect of preparation, so whenever they managed to tilt the game towards opening work, I would be found lacking. I would have done my labour but there would still be pieces missing and I didn't have the rigour in my analysis to detect what they were. Kasparov never allowed me any runs of form against him and always kept me trapped under immense opening pressure. Topalov too used that strategy. When Topalov was at 100 per cent, I found him hard to deal with. It took me a long time to learn to play him well. In 1996, he suddenly erupted, and it took me six months to stop losing to him. I won a couple of games after that, so it mitigated the feeling of total failure. There were years when he would lose games to me and there were others years when he would keep on beating me, so by the time we got to a World Championship match in 2010 I'd grown fairly consistent against him. By then, I'd cracked the code: If he made a half-mistake, I knew I had to cash in on it immediately. You have to be ready for a long struggle and once you're mentally prepared for that half your battle is won.

I also tended to prefer certain kinds of positions, the ones where a sudden crisis erupts, which I can instantly focus on over one that's on a slow boil and takes a while to unravel. Playing with tiny advantages, the kind of game that drags itself along till an opportunity arises, in fact, irked me. I was more the kind of player who liked to provoke a crisis and prevail. Soon, other players began to exploit that chink in my armour. Carlsen employed it against me at the 2013 World Championship, stalling me from getting into my favourite openings by insisting on playing long games. By this time, of course, my losing to him may have had a lot to do with our respective ages, but his strategy of making me play positions that I disliked also worked in his favour.

♛

The year I turned Grandmaster, 1988, was also the year I first used a computer for preparation. I received a computer as a gift in 1987 and had to leave it in Amsterdam with Albert Toby while the application seeking permission for it to be brought to India was being processed in New Delhi. It took roughly eight months for the sanction to come through and I finally flew back to India with it the next year. I had no chess software loaded on it, so I basically typed out moves one at a time. It was only four months later, when I visited Frederic in his home, that I realized that using the computer for chess was only effective when the software was at hand.

Late in the year, I bought a laptop, though I doubt if it would qualify as one today, what with its thick stand propping up a monstrously large screen. The good part was that suddenly all the information I wanted was packed into this one machine and I no longer needed to ferry around bulky books to tournaments. Since I could also use the computer to play games, the benefits seemed manifold. It was, however, a nightmare getting it cleared through Customs at the Madras airport. The country was a closed economy at the time and the Customs officials began by charging me a 250 per cent duty for bringing in the machine. They explained that while they understood it was a computer with chess software, if they had to classify it as chess equipment then chess would have to be the only purpose it served. But since it could be used to type out a letter, chess was certainly not its only use. The absurdity lay in the law, of course, and they were not in a position to ignore it. Eventually, I was allowed to bring the computer home, after some timely intervention by Manuel Aaron, who spoke to the Customs officials and also wrote critically about the incident in a national daily.

Though I was a part of the crossover generation that was bred on the chessboard and later migrated to computers, I was right at the top of the queue, using computers almost from the time they appeared in chess. ChessBase, a computer program stacked today with millions of games for anyone to access, was back then just a germ of an idea that Frederic, a chess fan, science journalist and academic, carried around in his head. In 1985, he designed the database along with Kasparov, then a young Grandmaster. A few months later, Frederic met Matthias Wüllenweber, a young physics student, and they went on to launch the company together. Incidentally, Frederic's mother was Goan Portuguese and he'd lived in India before his family moved to Germany when he was a teenager.

I first met Frederic in London, in 1987, when he was showing the program to a bunch of young players like me. I was 18 then. He asked me what my rating was and when I would be flying back to India. I was hovering around a mid-2500s Elo rating, and I told him as much. I added that I had a tournament in a week and couldn't afford to fly back to India right then. His next query was, 'So do you stay in a third-class hotel here?' I shook my head and with an absolutely straight face said, 'No, fourth class.' The cheeky reply fetched me an invitation to stay at his home in Hamburg any time I was around and check out the database for myself. I was not too used to taking favours and secretly wondered if the suggestion had been made in earnest. Eventually, my curiosity about the database won over my misgivings and, a few months after I'd met him, I called on his home telephone number, which he'd scribbled for me at the back of a book, and politely asked if his offer to have me over was still valid. He was more than happy to hear from me. He picked me up from the train station and drove me to his house in Hollenstedt, a suburb in Hamburg.

Frederic and his wife were in for a shock, though, when, close to mealtime, I dropped the unexpected bombshell that I was primarily a vegetarian. I had always been a non-fussy eater and, thanks to his Indian roots, Frederic pulled out a bottle of curry sauce and drizzled it over the vegetables they'd grilled to whip up a dish I could dig into. Immediately afterwards, they bought south Indian vegetarian cookbooks, and, in a few days' time, I was being fed spicy rasam-rice alongside a steady, daily diet of 200-odd games from the database. I devoured both. Frederic's young sons, Martin, then 11, and Tommy, four, hung around as I poked at the Atari ST, the first personal computer to offer a bitmapped colour graphical user interface, in their study. It came with an 8 Mhz Motorola 68,000 CPU and a mouse. One evening, I noticed Frederic staring at me curiously with a smile as I sat hunched before the computer, flipping through the database. I was holding the mouse upside down and yet it seemed to be working perfectly. He never forgets to retell this story no matter how many years have passed by.

Soon, over breakfast, I was pointing out errors in the database, the results that were wrong or mismatched. Frederic was keen that I make a note of all the errors. In many cases, the games were raw and unedited, so I grabbed a pen and gladly jotted them down from memory – the games, the results, the moves – and I could tell he was impressed.

During the 1993 World Championship match between Kasparov and Short, I bought a new fax machine. I kept it in my room in my parents' house in Madras and was mighty pleased with myself. I still needed someone to fax me the moves from games, though. We had two telephone lines at home for some reason and my father said I could reserve one exclusively for the fax machine. We had no idea it was illegal to do this. Apparently, you had to apply for a separate fax line if you wanted to operate a fax machine. I pestered Frederic to fax me the moves from the Short–Kasparov games and I recall receiving a paper with blots of ink in response. Worried, I picked up the phone, called Frederic in London and informed him that my machine didn't seem to be working. As it turned out, he was pulling a prank on me and promised to send me the moves soon.

Having details of games faxed over was one of the ways to beat geographical boundaries. The Soviet Union, so far, was in a yawning lead over the rest of the world when it came to chess – in experience and expertise – and access to information from there was considered the Holy Grail. It was about where you were placed in the information concentric circle. The closer to the inner circle you were (in this case, Moscow), the greater the quantum of information and the finest expertise that you had at your disposal, and as you moved further away, the information grew distant. The only way of getting it was to have the details of the games faxed to you, or tournament bulletins photocopied and brought to you by an acquaintance who was travelling to your part of the world. With technology butting in, waiting around for books that would earlier reach you once every few months by mail suddenly became irrelevant. Frederic sent me several floppies through a friend, one with the chess program I could install on my computer and the others with games on them. I later used the floppies as coasters.

We were soon talking about computers that were strong enough to beat any human, any Grandmaster, at a game. Access via computers took the rarity and exclusivity out of essential information, which now trickled down to all those seeking it. The advent of the Internet took this to a whole new level. You could now be in your home and yet be sparring with a Russian player online.

For the Candidates match against Kamsky the following year, I remember all of us – my mother, Maurice and Nieves, their son Eddie, and my trainers Ubilava and Yusupov – setting out from my Madrid home for Las Palmas. When it was almost time to board our flight, I suddenly felt I was missing something, and panicked when it struck me that I'd forgotten my laptop at home with all my match notes in it. At the time, I was lugging around a printer too, along with a wad of paper, so I could print out whatever I wanted my trainers to have a look at. I didn't seem to have forgotten that. Thankfully, our housekeeper, Maxi, had a key to my home. Maurice's daughter lived close to my place, so I telephoned her to get Maxi on the line and put the salvage plan to work. In the age of landlines you couldn't rattle off instructions like you do today, while someone has a phone plugged to the ear and is rummaging through a room in search of a misplaced object. But I managed to give Maxi precise directions. Once she'd located it, Eddie, who worked for the American multinational courier company FedEx, had it sent to Las Palmas, so I had it with me the same evening.

Gradually, the levellers that the chess world so keenly needed began to arrive on the scene. Chess engines, or computer programs that sift through and analyse numerous chess positions to offer concrete ways to solve a problem on the board, were among these. In the beginning the engines were ridiculously weak. They could see very little that you didn't. The way they approached a problem was to consider every possible move to counter it, but because they were not looking far enough they would sometimes offer the most ludicrous solutions. Initially, we used them just to check our work for any mistakes, the way mathematicians would use a calculator – to make sure there were no elementary errors and get the boring stuff out of the way. It left all the serious work for us to do. But slowly, with newer versions of the software, we began turning to it for more complex work. My initial response to engines was a certain amount of contempt. Gradually, however, the realization seeped in that even the weakest engine would occasionally spot something I had missed, perhaps because I had relaxed a bit or assumed the problem was over, didn't look hard enough or simply got lazy.

These were early days, in 1991, when we were using Fritz, a chess engine developed by the Dutch programmer Frans Morsch, which was added to ChessBase's database program. The first blow to the egos of human chess players came with this amazingly weak engine being able to point out a missing manoeuvre. In effect, as engines grew stronger, we had to concede more and more to them. Soon, we started running them with tactics, not to check whether we had made a mistake but simply to see what they had to offer as solutions or alternatives. The logical step that followed was to try to make sense of what they came up with.

For a long time after that, roughly over seven to eight years, human chess players were strategically a lot more superior to engines. The machines would often go wrong at a point where a long-term decision came into play. Humans could evaluate that correctly, while the engines worked aimlessly, trying to find a solution. Yet, often, even when we'd outplayed engines for long stretches in a game, we'd end up making a blunder here or a slip there at the final curve, and the machine would beat us.

Soon, it became clear that we are not better than the machines at anything. Even when they go down a blind alley once in a while, we no longer have the strength to beat them. With this realization becoming stronger over the years, the human chess players' ego has gradually dissipated. The hardest blows came in the beginning, when we were living in a bubble, convinced that chess was too difficult for anyone or anything other than human minds that were wired in a particular way. We were deluded into thinking that we were doing something unique. It turned out that chess is a game that can be reduced to a few rules and programs. On 11 May 1997, the IBM Supercomputer Deep Blue beat Kasparov in a six-game match under standard time controls. Kasparov had at the time raised doubts over it being a chess automation hoax and alleged that it may, after all, have been controlled by a human Grandmaster.

In my opinion, the entire episode was largely significant only to the world outside the ecosystem, where people were gasping over the game – and thus a unique function of the human mind – being conquered. This was the definitive moment, they proclaimed, that proved machines were superior to humans. We, the denizens of the chess world, knew it wasn't. It was more a milestone in public perception than on the chessboard. It was crucial since it was the first instance of a computer beating a World Champion in a match, but the games that were played weren't particularly impressive yet. It was also self-evident that you could play matches against Deep Blue and the result could be different. Kasparov had beaten it only a year before that, so it didn't make sense for his defeat a year later to be seen as the final verdict on computers taking over. The matches against computers also abruptly ceased at that point, making it more difficult to fathom whether or not the threat of computers being superior to humans and prospectively taking over was significant from a chess player's perspective. Within a few years of that, chess players began to acknowledge their fallibility and the seeming invincibility of computers.

In June 1999, I played Karpov in León, Spain, in an advanced game in which each player is teamed with a computer. It was intended to show how a human player and a computer working together could produce higher-quality games. I doubt we succeeded in doing that. As someone put it, 'It was Anand with a computer against Karpov with a high-tech scoresheet,' since the greater challenge for him seemed to be finding his way around using the computer. Karpov's methods can't really be held against him, because he belonged to the pre-computer era that found it difficult to simply flick a switch and adapt to the phenomenon. Karpov, for one, had never really worked with a computer and had trouble integrating his calculations with it. Even until late in his career, Karpov always had his notes written down on paper. He found them easier to absorb this way. The time limit was an hour to play all our moves, and he constantly lagged behind. I won 5–1. It was a wipeout because all I had to do was catch him in a position where he was vulnerable and let the computer take over. Karpov, on the other hand, struggled to enter a position and start an engine, and, at one point, the software sponsor left him a piece of paper with instructions on how to enter a move on the computer since he got trapped while making a move because he did not select it. He was caught with a machine that he didn't know how to get around.

A whole generation before Karpov, Efim Geller and David Bronstein, for instance, the real greats, were players whose analytical skills and ability to get to the heart of positions – which they did very much on their own, using traditional skills and brainwork – continue to amaze me. Their games will remind current players what it was like to solve positions unaided, but they had stopped playing many years before I played Karpov. Players from Karpov's generation remained in the circuit for a while because even though they were not proficient with computers, their brains didn't resist the new source of information and they were able to extract some value from the machines. To be honest, at times I too have found it extremely hard to work with computers. Still, since I'd spent only my teens without computers, I was flexible and adaptable, and made changes to the way I played my game. Had the same changes been hurled at me when I was in my 30s, I too may have struggled.

Watching Karpov and realizing what happens when you don't work with the best technology formed a part of my experience. Perhaps, at some level, it helped me embrace change. There are still moments when I fight new information, but over time I've made it a point to allow my brain to explore new methods and find ways to incorporate them in my work, because you simply have to keep up with new developments.

With access to more data, players today have the

opportunity to see more patterns and, if the eyes are trained to see them, it improves pattern recognition and the understanding of new positions. However, if the data is not understood, then its effect can be negative. If you simply look at a whole lot of variations without seeing a broader pattern or don't develop a fundamental understanding of what is happening in the larger landscape, then the data could be a burden rather than an aid. Complete dependence on data too is not desirable. For instance, notes on openings in chess today are vast and elaborate, but if a player simply throws himself at the mercy of the information and does not rehearse the actual lines and moves, he's unlikely to be able to use the information fruitfully in a real game. The key is to take in all the information and then work at the board to come up with a method to deal with the possible situations and put them into perspective.

During the 2007 World Championship tournament in Mexico, Nielsen came up with a novel idea and suggested we let our computers play against each other. So we switched on our engines, keyed in positions and left our computers to play overnight. The idea was to have the engines play out opening ideas relevant to us in order to check their value and draw inspiration from the games. In the morning, we'd scan the games it had generated for anything that we could take away for our preparation. To keep away from the glare of screens while we were asleep at night, we would leave the computers in the bathroom and keep the door slightly ajar so the machines wouldn't heat up. On one of the rest days during the tournament, Aruna and I were watching the absurdly hilarious Ben Stiller starrer *Zoolander* on my computer when it froze. Here we were in the middle of a tournament that would decide the World Champion and my computer, which had overheated from all the extensive games it had been playing, seemed to have crashed. We conducted a quick search on Google for a solution, and, as per the recommendations, held the laptop fan-end before the vent of the air conditioner, Aruna having voluntarily climbed a chair and a table to do this. This turned into a routine. Every day, after they played games for long hours, the computers were allowed a cool-off time in front of the AC vent. In the end, Nielsen's suggested experiment with our machines paid off, allowing us to generate ideas and build the confidence that came with the feeling of having put technology to good use.

This was unlike the 2010 World Championship match in Sofia, when we'd felt helpless in the face of the rumour that my opponent, Topalov, had access to a computer cluster with 112 cores of frighteningly superior hardware and that it was running the latest program of the chess engine Rybka 4. I couldn't even visualize at the time what kind of assistance the supercomputer could offer Topalov, because I'd never worked with something that powerful. What hadn't struck us at that time was that it wasn't about how 'super' the computer was but about the ability of the software to utilize every bit of its power. The other (and more crucial) question was whether a faster car takes you somewhere that a slower car does not, or does it simply take you there quicker? A faster car that doesn't take you somewhere different is, well, just a faster car. The scenario was pretty similar with a supercomputer and regular hardware.

When it comes to data, though, the need for discretion takes centre stage. 'The more, the better' certainly isn't a clever principle to swear by. There is little use in having a lot of information if it leads you to confusion about the choice you should be making. Many of the most beautiful games I've played have come about at a time when I knew very little and had just one strategic theme or a clear goal I was aiming to achieve. It's important to have accurate information (even if there's less of it) than be avalanched and confused by a sheer abundance of it.

My win against Fabiano Caruana in August 2017 in the Sinquefield Cup at St. Louis comes to mind here. I played the English Opening, which was an unusual and surprise choice since I'd used it sparingly in my career. Caruana responded by using a line I wasn't familiar with. Soon, it was clear that all the data apart, we just had to get down to playing the good old game in the old-fashioned way – using our instincts and experience-driven strategy. I was relentless in my attack on the Black king despite Caruana's rook nesting on the seventh rank and posing a threat to my queen. I soldiered on, exposing his king to heavy fire. The final move of the sequence, where my queen on the d4 square walked in, open to capture by the black rook on d8, was enough for me to wrap up the game. Caruana had clearly missed it. In that instance, it was important for me not to get fixated on the nagging fact that I didn't have any special preparation in place. It turned out to be one of the prettiest games I'd ever played.

With the recent entrance of artificial intelligence into the scene, there's a fresh level of unknowns to contend with.

The primary task is to comprehend what has changed with AI and the areas that continue to be untouched by its existence. Computers can be seen as a continuum of what books were in terms of organizing information – only that they perhaps do so at a superior level and by using different means. In adapting to these means, one has to alter one's skills. When I had books, I would look at the diagrams, try to process the information, mentally develop a picture of what was accurate and go to the board to play a game with that visual floating in my head. With computers and databases this process sped up, became more organized and increased the volume of information being made available, so that the ease of accessing it was balanced by the increasing workload. Here, we arrived at a fresh paradigm.

Much of what people say about AI changing the world sounds incredibly similar to the rhetoric on old-style computer programs when they burst upon the scene. Computers showed chess players scenarios we couldn't see for ourselves or hadn't tried to fathom in human terms, but they weren't free from roadblocks. In chess-player jargon, the evaluation of the positions would often be stuck at 0.001, which is the difference in the evaluation of pawns and essentially implies that the position is flat. When the old-style program hit this barrier, it would just stop and nothing interesting would happen for some time. Every once in a while, it would wake up on its own, but essentially, unless you thought for yourself and kept suggesting moves to it, it hit some sort of performance wall.

There is a vast qualitative difference with AI in the picture. Its beauty lies in that idea of self-learning from examples without prior knowledge, which eliminates human biases and intervention. It took AI's program AlphaZero just four hours from being fed with nothing but the rules of the game for it to destroy the highest-rated chess engine Stockfish in a 1,000-game match. It's a testament to AI's extraordinary ability to master gameplay.

At the cost of oversimplification, what AI does is to remove the loss of information that would occur when we tried to capture and explain in words the essence of intuitive play. It does this by allowing programs to learn for themselves after feeding in just the rules and then letting them play against themselves. In a way, AI is showing us details and hidden nuances that older computers would offer us only if we pointed them in the right direction. It's opening up many new doors, new areas that we can mine, bringing back to life areas we thought were dead or that we were bored with, which explains the excitement about it.

Inevitably, AI will approach a lot of problems differently and it is possible that this will revolutionize chess again. As it stands now, we're being offered a whole lot of new information and a host of fresh conclusions – and we are left with the tiny question of dealing with them. One way to do this is to apply the lessons we took away from the computer revolution – wholeheartedly trying to understand the conclusions that don't make sense to us in the beginning instead of rejecting them outright, or even accepting them without question. Computers are constantly churning out exceptions to every rule we knew. Lowering the resistance to change, removing bias from the picture, keeping an open mind and being willing to adapt is the best way to hit the ground running. It's essentially the attitude I've come to adopt. Dogmas and judgements, I've learnt, have to be shed in favour of facts. This has allowed me to become more open-minded and occasionally re-evaluate my views. It's helped me evolve and stay relevant through every wave of change.

My current trainer, Grzegorz Gajewski, began using AI about four or five months before I did, in 2017, and raved so much about how amazing it was that I had to take a look. I was attracted to the new AI material because Stockfish had been beaten comprehensively by it and many of the games that had been played were incredibly interesting. Others too had started to study them. A bit later, AI appeared on our computers through Leela Chess Zero, a strong engine that could run on decent hardware, which Gajewski brought to my attention around the end of 2018.

For the moment, we're using old-style systems as well as AI, and it's actually very interesting when the results from both differ, because that's when you can learn the most, since only one of them can be right.

Increasingly, the efforts required are less. I can switch on an engine, leave it for a while, watch a movie and then come back and see what the engine has done, because it will have the right conclusions. My job starts at this point – to understand the conclusions at a fine granular level. The positions I can learn to navigate and the ease with which I can recall them when the need arises – that's the skill set I bring to a game.

Presently, we are in a situation where things are

potentially in churn. Rating lists could get scrambled. We could possibly have a whole generation that will see the chessboard in a completely different light since we are now able to view games and trends that hadn't occurred to us or hadn't been tried out before. Unlike having one computer in an IBM laboratory somewhere which can beat the World Champion, now pretty much everyone with a computer and access to AI can give themselves the odds of doing the same.

The way we should deal with it is by asking ourselves a few questions: What are the new things I can learn from this? What are the old things I should unlearn? What have I understood well enough that I can apply to my games going forward? It's not enough to have half-truths whispered in our ears, like the old Oracle whose answers we may have understood without knowing why. There will inevitably be a learning curve while we get better at applying these lessons, but in chess terms this progress is really exciting. The old-style programs had reached a stage where the information they were generating had everyone more or less equally placed. AI is threatening to unbalance it again. The story goes that Caruana and Carlsen began using AI at least six months before everyone else, since they were preparing for their match in November 2018. It's not about access any more – that aspect is getting equalized incredibly fast. Everything is on cloud, so you can rent it, or friends who have access to it are able to lend it to you. Unlike earlier, junior players now have access to essentially the same hardware as the seniors. It could be that the top players are buying incredibly expensive high-end hardware, but almost any chess player has access to something that is good enough, so the difference is miniscule. The eventual differentiator, as with most technology, will not be what hardware you have at home, but what use you are able to make of it.

Levon Aronian v. Viswanathan Anand (0–1)
(White)   (Black)

Round 4, 2013 Tata Steel Chess Tournament, Wijk aan Zee

BLACK WINS

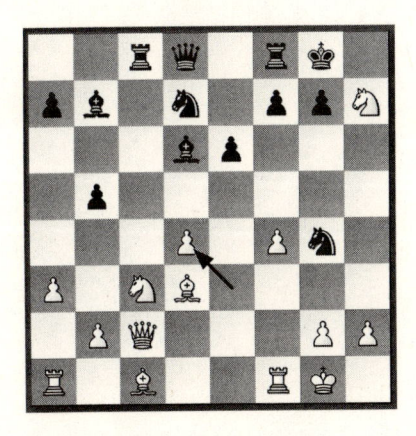

For the sheer beauty of the motives, I would say this is probably the best game I've played in my life. I had not anticipated the line, and though I remembered the evaluation, the details were hazy. Since the line had been checked by my team, I decided to invest the time necessary to find the right move. A tiny nuance occurred to me – that the knight had eventually come to d3. I spent 30 minutes working out a way to get it there because I knew that even if I had very little time for the remaining moves, once I found the way forward and cracked the idea, everything else would fall into place.

♛

In any situation in life, being adaptable is the only way to grow and succeed. You may have skills that you've perfected, a certain worldview that worked for you at a particular stage – but the reality is that circumstances change, and you can't be prepared for everything. Lowering your resistance to change, removing bias and being willing to adapt will help you tackle whatever comes your way. Once you've assessed the resources at your disposal and weighed what is feasible against what is risky you will see the path.

NINE

B♛NN AGAIN

FINDING BEAUTY IN RISK

14 OCTOBER 2008. ARUNA AND I SAT MOTIONLESS AS SHE PATIENTLY waited for me to make my first move to the door of our hotel room, Suite 344, at the Hilton Bonn. I had ticked off a 45-minute nap and my pre-match snack from my to-do list. My schedule on the first day of a World Championship match is usually squirmy, with both my mind and my body trying to settle in and pick a routine that can last through a fortnight. That morning, I'd woken up at 9 a.m., had my breakfast and hopped over to the training room for a survey of the battle plans drawn up by my four seconds – Nielsen, Rustam, Surya and Radek. We'd stayed locked in for two hours, panicking over our revisions, before I returned to my room for a nap, showered, took quick bites of a banana and washed it down with a chocolate milkshake. When tension is stabbing at you with a bowie knife, the mind and stomach refuse to process the idea of a meal. Food then should turn both inconspicuous and effortless, a sandwich or wrap, or a banana and milkshake. Having run through my schedule,

there was now nothing left for me to do but leave for the tournament venue.

The Bonn Federal Art Gallery, 15 minutes away from the hotel, was to be the setting of what could be the biggest match of my life. Since Kasparov's retirement in 2005, the bragging rights for the world's best player had been up for grabs. Kramnik, Topalov and I were the primary contenders, but none of us had sufficiently proven ourselves to be better than the other two yet. Eleven months ago, I'd become the World Champion in the Mexico tournament, with Kramnik in second place. He'd been disparaging of my worthiness then, and suggested he'd only lent me the title temporarily and that I'd have to earn it in the match against him in Bonn. Though we were sworn rivals in the sport, we were never bitter towards each other. We were just two people who wanted the same thing. Most of the time, he was good company and I would occasionally give him a call during tournaments we were both playing in to check if he wanted to step out to grab a bite.

For this match, though, our regular relationship was on standby and we were more frigid than cordial with each other. It had suddenly reached the stage at which everything that the other person does bothers you no end. Six months ago, at the Amber Tournament in Monte Carlo, I'd beaten him in one game with Black, but my mind had been scattered following that encounter. I hated being there and all I could think of was our impending match in Bonn. Just having him around unsettled me.

At the end of the World Championship match in Mexico about a year ago, I'd decided to follow my gut and pick risk over familiarity. I'd already tried the alternative – languishing in familiar terrain for too long – and suffered its terrifying after-effects in Dortmund in 2001. I was too cocooned in my game, overlooking the gaps in my repertoire, sticking to tried and tested systems and methods, veering away from risks. It was easily one of the worst tournaments I'd played, in which, without the thrill of a risk or the spark of a fresh idea that I could try at the board, every day had seemed like unending drudgery.

Immediately after my Mexico win, we'd moved into our new home in Chennai. Life in Collado Mediano had been strikingly lonely. It was a small town with limited access to services and we barely knew anyone around even after living there for a while. Maurice and Nieves were our family, and following Nieves's death in May 2004, we felt even more alone. I was no longer working with Ubilava and the Internet invasion had turned the world flatter, so there was no pressing need to stay on in Spain either. Meanwhile, in India, the chess scenario was livening up, and I was in regular touch with national players like Sandipan Chanda and Surya. We'd only seen photographs of our new home in RA Puram before we bought it. On the day we were moving in, a television crew landed up to interview me. It was funny because the crew wanted to record a tour of our home on camera while we tried to figure out the electric switches and arrangements in various rooms.

I'd also begun building my team for the match from the beginning of 2008. Nielsen had been working with me intermittently, often via email, since the early 2000s, even while Ubilava had been my full-time trainer. During the

2005 San Luis World Championship tournament, a double round robin featuring the top eight players, Ubilava had agreed to a camp with another player and couldn't be with me. Problems had been cropping up between us before that and our relationship was slightly strained by then. From that tournament onwards, Nielsen came on board as my main second. It was a timely partnership. At the time, I was struggling to keep pace with the innovations in computers and in games being played. Nielsen had encyclopaedic knowledge and was updated on everything to do with chess, right from the latest software to interesting ideas he'd struck upon in obscure Danish school tournaments, and complemented me perfectly.

He suggested we add Rustam, who had won the World Championship title from the FIDE cycle in 2004, to the team. It was a good idea since we needed someone who had competed at a high level. Once we got together, I learnt that Rustam had another quality. Younger than me by 10 years, he was the guy who could give me the unvarnished hard truth about my game, crack a dirty joke and lighten the mood, and also deliver a pep talk when I doubted myself. Where Nielsen was more likely to say, 'You'll be fine, don't worry,' Rustam would put it as 'You'll kick his a** today' or direct at me a more-than-mild rebuke like 'show some b***s' if I began to have misgivings about my performance. Both of them were completely conversant with computers, and with modern methods creeping into games around then they made for absolutely priceless trainers. I ran into Radek, then 21, at a Bundesliga match in December 2007. While I was preparing to play him and skimming over his previous games, it struck me that he had deep, creative opening ideas and that the 1.d4 was his zone of operation. I took his email id and, a few weeks later, wrote to him asking if he'd be willing to work with me. He promptly agreed. I also wanted an Indian player as the fourth member of my team and Surya fit the bill. The previous year he'd come over to my house in Madras after having qualified for the World Cup and we'd looked at a couple of variations together. I was impressed by his understanding of the game and, later, over Skype, asked him if he'd be interested in joining us. Once he hopped on board, my team was complete.

I had decided in an inspired moment after my win in Mexico to switch from the 1.e4 opening, which was my comfort zone, and revolve my preparatory plans around Kramnik's own signature 1.d4 opening for this match. The 1.e4, I knew, was the rug I was expected to curl into. It's what Kramnik would anticipate I'd play, lay his traps beautifully and then pull the rug from under me in one swift motion. My scheme was both to throw him off and take him on in his den. We knew it could turn out to be either a masterstroke or a howler, but I had resolved to stick with my decision.

My team and I had thus pounded on with our ambush plans for close to half a year at my home in Bad Soden. In the last few weeks before the match, we were suddenly struck by a fresh problem: What if Kramnik played the 1.e4 to begin with? Alarm and trepidation set in. We tried to rehearse lines, bounce around systems and realized we didn't have a solid defence to it. In focusing all my efforts and resources at surprising him, it was possible that I had left my flank completely exposed. The only consolation was that it was an opening I'd played all my life, so the possibility of being able to conjure up something impromptu at the board if he did use it against me wasn't totally remote.

Back in the hotel room, the moment of truth was upon us. I rose to my feet, dragged myself to the door and reached for the knob. My hands were trembling, frozen. Aruna, only too relieved that I'd finally made the long walk, turned the knob and let us out.

Kramnik had tried to mess with my head on the day of the opening ceremony by springing a surprise and announcing that my former second Leko was now on his team. He hoped perhaps that it would bother me, but I hadn't worked with Leko in nine years, so I didn't feel he had violated any ethical boundaries. Moreover, it was a good opportunity for Leko and I didn't think it was reasonable for me to expect him to turn down a work opportunity or demand loyalty unless I was guaranteeing him a job. So I was neither shocked nor hurt. Since I had already decided on switching openings, I knew Kramnik's team would probably end up spending more time working on the dead-end alleys, so I just did a double take for 10 seconds and then shrugged off the news. It was, however, hard for me not to note that this was the beginning of a trend that saw friends showing up in the enemy camp.

In the first game, when Kramnik pushed his queen's pawn two squares for a 1.d4 opening, I could almost imagine four fully grown men back in the training room leaping with joy. Our worst fear had dissipated. Somewhere deep down, I was certain Kramnik wouldn't switch from his usual favourite opening, but now that the move was made I could finally breathe easy. We went on to agree to a quick draw, and I returned to the workroom where my team sat amid a sea of cables and bottomless cups of coffee, with the beats of Coldplay's 'Viva La Vida' thrumming against its walls.

We were now at the threshold of the crucial second game. I was to play 1.d4 from the White side. Having known Kramnik, I had an understanding of how organized and systematic he was in his work. I was certain he'd drawn up a neat list of all the lines he should run a check on and 1.d4 most certainly would be a part of it. However, I had a feeling that he was unlikely to take that part of the work seriously – much like my attitude had been towards a defence for 1.e4. When you've played an opening for two decades of your life, it's hard to tell yourself there could be a surprise in store and make your brain earnestly prepare for it afresh. During game 2, when I played the opening and looked up at Kramnik's face, it was undisturbed. He wasn't quite falling off his chair. I ran into a bit of a time trouble and a complex position, so when he offered a draw I took it. Two draws in two games and I knew this was turning out just like I'd imagined – a battle of attrition.

Playing 1.d4 against Kramnik was hugely satisfying for me. By using his dominant choice of opening against him, I was almost forcing him to fight himself. In pressure situations, this kind of approach brings with it a high probability of success. In this case, it certainly carried the threat, however pint-sized, that I may have hit upon that one single thing that he hadn't run a check on – and that could be enough to ruin his day.

A non-chess cue too hinted that my gut instinct about

taking a fresh path wasn't entirely misplaced. I had an impending lecture at the Madras Management Association (MMA) in Chennai soon after the Mexico tournament, and the notes I'd drawn up for myself abounded in my views on the benediction of risk-taking. I found myself thinking, 'So am I really going to stand before a roomful of smart people and advise them on the benefits of taking risks, when I myself fear the slightest change in my openings?' My willingness to play the 1.d4 also allowed me to enter the White games with more enthusiasm than I would otherwise have while navigating the staid familiarity of 1.e4. I have always enjoyed having fresh problems on the board – and there is something to be said for not trying to be too clever, but just going into a game with the attitude of wanting to enjoy it.

When you take a decision and stick to it, it gives your team a lot of clarity. When your path is clear before you and you own responsibility for the call you've made, everyone around you is put at ease. Your team is then assured they don't have to hesitate and can confidently apply their expertise to the situation. That's how it was with the 1.d4. I made it quite clear to my seconds that they should do what was required and the consequences of my decisions would be borne by me alone. This freed them up. Obviously, our attitude was also conditioned by the fact that it was our first match together as a team, and our enthusiasm towards taking risks and preparing for them paid off in spades. I may give the impression of being a guy who lives in Zen-like calm and could well be rolling prayer wheels at a monastery, but the truth is that I savour taking risks and jumping off the high board. My favourite pastimes reflect this. I find little else as exhilarating as the feeling of being one with the clouds and the sky while paragliding and feeling the sea spray on my face as I wind-surf or take off on a jet-ski, chasing the waves on holidays. Las Palmas in the Canary Islands has always been my favourite destination to tick off my bucket list brimming with my cravings for adventure.

One of the ideas that came up late in our preparatory months in the run-up to the championship was Rustam's novel take on the bread-and-butter Semi-Slav Defence. He had used it against Gelfand a year earlier. It seemed to unbalance the position nicely. At that time, it was just one out of 10 things that Kramnik may have looked at, but it appeared to be a good one to harness and bring the game into my territory. We fell in love with the line, but also realized that it may need a lot of work to weather the storm of a World Championship match. We named it Kasim's Meran 'baby' since it was his idea. The Meran took its nomenclature from the South Tyrol city, formerly part of Austria but later given to Italy, and renamed Merano after World War I. The city hosted a tournament in 1924 in which Rubinstein used the Meran System as Black to beat Ernst Grünfeld. The funny thing was every time we would think it was working well and that we had it under control, one of my team members would run a double-check and break the news to us that the whole line had fallen apart. Clearly, by nature, it wasn't a stable line and making it stick was a bit like walking a tightrope. What was worrying was that even after we reached Bonn, the problems with the line didn't cease.

It was in the third game that I decided to let the Meran

'baby' loose and went over the lines with Surya one final time, an hour before the game. It seemed to work. When I executed it at the board, Kramnik walked into the main line and I had him just where I wanted – neck-deep in a complex position, far removed from his beloved dry, technical positions. My novelty on move 17, Rg4, bringing together the defence of the d4 pawn with the flocking of the pieces on the kingside, raised the tension of the position and forced us to walk a tightrope. I went on to break through with my most crucial win in the 12-game match. The momentum had been wrested.

At the end of the drawn fourth game, I walked into the training room and noticed that both Surya and his worktable were missing. I was told he was feeling unwell, and wanted to work out of his own room. In reality, he had been diagnosed with chicken pox and was in quarantine so that the rest of us wouldn't contract it. This was, however, not divulged to me until he recovered and rejoined the team later.

Through the entire rest day preceding the fifth round, up until midnight, the Meran kept breaking down. There was also some debate within the team over whether I should repeat it at all. I decided in favour of it since I felt it fell in place with our risk-seeking theme for the match and if it worked, it could help extend my lead to a handy two points.

On the afternoon of the game, I showered, got dressed and sat down for a final review with my team. The game was just an hour away, but the scenario around the Meran was still slightly cloudy, the line still offering trouble. No sooner had our car driven away from the hotel than it struck me that my mind had gone blank and I needed a quick revision. Aruna tried calling Radek but found his phone switched off. We then called everyone else, with no luck. Typically, the time I was away playing was the only window the team got to shower and catch up on sleep before they logged in to work through another night. I tried telling myself that I should not think of it as an ill omen, but such thoughts are difficult to keep away from one's mind when so much is at stake.

We reached the venue, my mind still unsettled, although in my heart of hearts I knew that even if one of them called back, I had no time to take in and process any information they gave me. In what seemed to be a second sign, I came upon a jammed entrance door at the venue. I shrugged it off and proceeded to the board. Thankfully, Kramnik was ready with a serving of news that brought me relief. He repeated his 1.d4 opening despite the catastrophe it had brought him in the third game and opened up the path for me to unleash the Meran again. He really enjoyed confronting this line, which was lucky for us because we had done a lot of specific work on it and were happy to accept the risks it held for the rewards it promised. Besides, it's always pleasing to have your opponent bite the bait. This is perhaps the greatest beauty of risk-taking. You never know the mistakes your opponent may be capable of unless you put yourself out there and take a chance.

In this instance, my positive attitude to the match was a bonus. Had I lost, perhaps my mind would have tried to join the dots between everything that had gone wrong leading up to the match and created a portrait of unavoidable doom. But when you have a good result, all such thoughts go out of the window. Of course, the team back at the hotel was in for a panic attack when they eventually checked their phones, and were put at ease only after they learnt of the match result. They never switched off their phones again for as long as we played together.

For this match we had also gained an edge from our access to the software Rybka 3, which we had installed on our machines and then connected them to multiple powerful computers around the world. It allowed us to use the hardware without it being physically present in our workspace and offered us the advantage of mining sharp variations for an analytical edge.

In the last five games, I held my position. Even though I could technically afford to, I did not become too defensive. I struggled a bit after game 7 and the draws were not the breeziest. Every time I played risky lines and got away with them, I felt like I'd braved danger and emerged unscathed. In a match situation, it's important to keep the fight alive. I ended up taking a whole lot of risks – sometimes even unnecessary ones – with White in the ninth game and ran into trouble. But when you've reached this stage, the idea is not to play passive and allow a negative predisposition to seep in.

When Surya rejoined us at the end of game 7, following his isolated stay, everything around him had changed. I had a massive three-point lead over Kramnik, and Radek, whom we could never get to agree to a sushi meal, was proffering suggestions for Japanese restaurants. The lead was a luxury and I began to think the match was over. The greatest danger of a premature celebratory mood is that it might distract you and lead you to falter. There is a huge difference between having an overwhelming margin and the arbiter actually stopping the clock and you signing the scoresheet. Some things just aren't over till they're over. In these moments, when you're gloating over a lead or a win before it happens, as though it were a mere formality, it's important to find a goal that will propel you onwards, because even if you're leading all it takes is one moment of carelessness in one game to plunge you into trouble. Every advantage you have can be chipped away slowly, and if you're not mindful of your present and are busy visualizing future celebrations, then you may not eventually quite be a part of it.

I'd been scalded by my haste in the past. After two initial draws during the 1994 Candidates quarter-final match against Kamsky in Sanghi Nagar, Hyderabad, I'd won the next two games to take an imposing 3–1 lead. I ended up relaxing too early, deducing that the match was within my reach. Matters rapidly slipped from my grasp and from being tied 4–4, I went on to lose both rapid play-offs. There was also the subtext of all the social courtesies that I was expected to grant during the match since it was happening in India. Since I was bad at saying no to granting favours, I was sucked into a whirlpool of distractions. This, combined with my lackadaisical attitude following the lead, undid me.

Though we were heading into game 11 against Kramnik with a two-point cushion, losing the tenth game meant we needed to concentrate and get the job over with, or the match could spin out of our control. Opening preparations typically revolve around finding an advantage. In this case, all we had to do was look for a lifeless position and find a path to a draw. There are dangers to being too passive, though. In fact, the worst thing is to be close to a draw and yet not be certain that it will actually come about. When that happens, you're so eager for a draw that you start making bad moves. My team had it worked out. The idea was to have a simple preparation in place. They also came up with the blandest positions where nothing could go wrong, a forced line that ends in a draw, which I was just expected to toe.

We also knew that Kramnik wouldn't opt for the kind of line that would allow me to force a draw. I knew I was dealing with a kamikaze fighter here. Kramnik was desperate. Anything less than a win in the round and it would all be over for him. I decided, therefore, to switch back to the familiar comfort of my turf, 1.e4. Kramnik didn't seem to have anticipated that I'd switch back to 1.e4 and chose the Najdorf variation himself, which threw up a bunch of drawing options for White. At some point during the game, I sensed he'd given up. It's an emotion I recognize because I've felt it so many times myself – in a tournament that's going badly for you, you just try to salvage something. Towards the end, I forced myself to keep still and not give away how anxiously I was waiting for a draw. Any time that Kramnik wanted a draw he'd find an outstretched arm ready to take his offer. But my brain barked, 'C'mon be serious, just concentrate.' My team had ordered me not to play even a minute more than was necessary and they faced no resistance from me on that count. When Kramnik offered me a draw, I restrained myself from grabbing it. I collected my thoughts, paused for a few seconds just to enjoy the moment, and did a mental waltz before agreeing to it.

I met Aruna backstage, and she asked, 'So…?' We'd grown into a couple who finished each other's sentences. I smiled and said, 'It's over!' Spent, we hugged, not knowing what else to do.

I learnt only later that my feverish state and aching muscles during the final two games had to do with particulars beyond the tension of a finish and the exhilaration of a win. Surya had generously passed on the chicken pox virus to both Aruna and me. Thankfully, by the time we were covered in full-blown blisters, the match was over.

Back in the hotel, my team, wrung dry of their final reserves of energy, hugged, cheered and flagged down a cab to join me at the venue. Afterwards, we trooped down to an Indian restaurant for dinner and the owner, courtesy his south Indian roots, happily whipped up dreamy, delightful dosas for us. That evening, the champagne tasted like heaven.

Vladimir Kramnik v. Viswanathan Anand (0–1)
(White)   (Black)

Game 3, 2008 World Championship, Bonn
BLACK WINS

Rg4 was one of the star moves of this game. Moves like these are difficult to find on the board, and even when you find them, it's easy to disbelieve they're there. Here, it was particularly special because it allowed me to apply the work we'd done over months of preparation. It's true that it's impossible to anticipate everything on the board, and I had to find my way around the situation. But it helped immensely to have a head start. The later games increased my lead, but this was the game in which I broke through. I think of it as one that might have won the match for me.

♛

The lead this game gave me was a luxury, but I restrained myself from celebrating too quickly. I'd suffered from the consequences of doing that earlier – relaxing when I should have been focused, or letting the excitement of an anticipated win take over. There is a difference between having an overwhelming lead and actually finishing a game on top. In these moments, it's important to be acutely mindful of your present, find calm and keep yourself grounded. If you're too busy visualizing future success it may eventually give you the slip.

TEN

THE ADVERSITY ADVANTAGE

A VOLCANIC ASH CLOUD, A ROAD TRIP
AND A TITLE

THE DAY WAS GROWING MORE DISQUIETING BY THE HOUR. FLIGHTS had been grounded, Nielsen and Radek were yet to find a way to reach Frankfurt, and we had no idea how we'd make it to Sofia in time for my World Championship match against Topalov. We'd heard some rumblings about an Icelandic volcano spewing ash. Yet, when we looked up at the sky, it was the clearest, brightest, most beautiful shade of blue we'd ever seen. It spelt hope. Or so we believed.

It was already 15 April 2010 and the match was now just a little more than a week away. I found no reason to shuffle my team, which had brought me one of my most splendid career wins in Bonn two years earlier.

For the match, our original plan was for the entire team to assemble at our home in Bad Soden, 18 kilometres away from Frankfurt, and fly out to Sofia together on 16 April. Aruna and I had flown to Frankfurt from Madrid a day earlier. Surya, who took the last flight out of India before all

Europe-bound operations from the country were suspended, and Rustam, had already reached Bad Soden. But now, with the ash cloud hanging heavy over us, air travel was out of the question. Nielsen was dealing with an avalanche of cancellations – first his plane and then the train he managed to book himself on were pulled out of service. Finally, he had a friend drive him from the Danish city of Aarhus to Hamburg, following which he took a train to Frankfurt. Radek too somehow managed a complicated train journey from Warsaw to Frankfurt.

I was mildly aware of the pangs of panic that surrounded me, but wasn't yet an earnest part of it. Tutankhamun had my attention instead. I was caught in a phase of reading up on Egyptian history. Aruna probably thought I was a raving lunatic to be lounging in our living room, my limbs in full stretch, reading up on a fourteenth-century BCE pharaoh when our travel plans for a match that had me defending my World Championship title had hit a wall. By nature, I tend to be unhurried and unruffled by things that appear to be beyond my control. You could plonk me in the busiest queue at an airport counter and the collective angst to get ahead would rarely splice its way through to me. Typically, when we ran late for our flights to India from Madrid, Aruna would negotiate her way up the queue, cajoling people ahead of her telling them that she had to travel to a far-off South Asian country. Awkward about joining her in the proceedings, I'd be content to stand at a distance, lost in a chess book or a puzzle, without a care in the world. Only when she'd cracked her way through would she find me beside her at the counter.

While we managed to get ourselves rebooked on an evening flight scheduled to leave on 16 April, the signs were now growing ominous. When you have absolutely nothing to do but wait, the day tends to go by very slowly. Practice games and studying variations were out of the question. Unpacking computers and equipment didn't seem like a tempting idea since we were weighing the possibility of a sudden travel plan emerging out of nowhere. We treaded water and waited for a resolution.

News began trickling in of airport after airport shutting down and matters quickly began to get jumpy. It was still unclear whether our evening flight would depart at all and the threat of Frankfurt airport too shuttering itself loomed large. On the counsel and assistance of one of our close friends Eric van Reem, who worked for the German carrier Lufthansa, Aruna managed to collect our baggage – that had been checked through from Madrid – from the Frankfurt airport. It turned out to be a timely move since, within a few hours, chaos and typically arcane security processes kicked in, and the airport shut down. We couldn't be certain of what lay in store, but it was now growing evident that there wasn't going to be an easy solution. The alternate mode of transport, trains, would take at least 28 hours and were already overbooked.

Wolfgang Grenke, one of the main sponsors of the Bundesliga team Baden-Baden, whom I represented in the German league games, was kind enough to offer us his private jet, but getting clearance to fly was almost impossible. (Of course, we weren't the only ones whose plans were stalled by volcanic ash drifting across Europe's skies. Neither were we the most distinguished. While I had a World Championship match to get to, then US President Barack Obama had to scrap his travel plans to attend the funeral of Polish President Lech Kaczynski ánd his wife Maria in Krakow after they were killed in an unfortunate air crash.)

The only plausible option left for us now was to travel by road. But this too was becoming complicated – car rental and taxi services were running short on both vehicles and personnel, and rates were quadrupling. Most wouldn't agree to drive all the way to Bulgaria. Once again, Eric used his influence and ties in the travel industry to get through to a service, Taxi Lagerberg, in Amstelveen. They were willing to depute two drivers with a Mercedes Sprinter van to drive down from the Dutch city 500 kilometres away, pick us up from Bad Soden on 18 April, and drive us to Sofia.

On the evening of 17 April, once we had our travel plans in place, it struck Aruna that we could enforce the 'force majeure' clause mentioned in the match contract and seek a postponement. It would buy us a few days' time for our road journey. She called our legal counsel back in India, who agreed it was a good idea, and Aruna quickly jotted down the notice we could serve FIDE as he dictated it to her. According to article 8.2 of the agreement, I didn't even have the benefit of the seven-day period that the contract stipulated for acclimatizing to the conditions. FIDE knew it didn't have any grounds to refuse us, but the Bulgarians in the organizing committee were bitter over our request and termed it both 'derogatory and unacceptable'.

Chess players thrive on detail, the hows, whys and

wherefores of things. We love a whole-board view. Whenever I picked up on a snatch of conversation between Aruna and FIDE, I ended up probing her for more information. Both of us soon realized it wasn't a good idea – her arguing with the officials and haggling for time in what was already a stressful scenario, and me ruminating over certain disturbing snippets I'd caught. We arrived at an agreement that Aruna would handle the issue entirely by herself with no further questions asked till it was resolved. Only once we received written communication from the FIDE officials accepting our force majeure clause and expressing their willingness to offer a postponement did we board our minibus.

Driving through Serbia was the quickest route, but since Aruna, Surya and I weren't residents of the European Union, and our Schengen visas, which allow travel between European countries, weren't valid in the east European nation, we settled for a detour that would have us traversing roughly 2,000 kilometres across four countries – Austria, Hungary, Romania and into Bulgaria. Thankfully, our drivers checked with us on this in time, a detail likely to have been overlooked in a minibus packed with Europeans (apart from my seconds, Eric too joined us on our journey).

We set out at 11.30 a.m. on Sunday, 18 April, in the eight-seater equipped with a DVD player, two screens and a fridge we'd stocked with fruits, chocolate milk, chocolate bars and Coke. We were to cross the German border in Passau, drive through Austria and stay overnight at Budapest. The weather and idyllic surroundings were almost handpicked for a road trip. We were besotted with Vienna. Rolling mountains, lilacs and tulips in bloom, puffballs of white and pink blossoms, and young parents with kids on strollers on the sidewalk were everywhere we looked. The quiet, grey winter months had made way for spring and the atmosphere was celebratory in every way. It's hard to get yourself to do serious work when there are such beauteous, sweeping landscapes unfolding outside. We played magnetic chess, discussed lines in Catalan on Nielsen's small tablet PC, and huddled around for marathon sessions of the television series *House*, having abandoned our ambitious plans of getting a whole lot of work done. We'd decided, rather, to make a fun road trip of it. Since Aruna and I had visited Budapest the previous year, she had the contact of a hotel in ready reckoning and managed to book four rooms for the night.

It didn't help that Topalov's team was anything but sympathetic of our bizarre circumstances. It may have been too much to hope that they wouldn't try to take advantage of our predicament, but we'd expected them to be at least moderately accommodating. Earlier, even as we were wondering how we'd reach Sofia, the Bulgarian sports minister had informed the local press that I had already arrived. Even as Aruna sat in the back seat of the van and called FIDE and the Indian Chess Association in turn, negotiating and seeking help on firming up the number of days of the postponement, there were news reports being run that we were luxuriating in the Bulgarian capital and simply giving the organizers a hard time with our story of being on the road. Aruna had the challenging task at hand of sounding both upset and stern to the people at the other end of the line, while keeping up an undisturbed facade and a low tone so as not to throw the team into a panic.

We reached Budapest at 10.30 p.m., gorged on Thai food at a restaurant opposite our hotel and retired for the night. The next morning, just before we checked out, we turned on the television in our room and learnt that the Vienna airport had shut down only a day ago, not earlier, as we had believed. The arbiter for the match had managed to catch a flight out of the city just before the airport closed down. I couldn't help but feel helpless over the situation we were stuck in and prayed I wouldn't be treated to the sight of a plane flying over my head just as we entered Sofia at the end of a long road trip. We drove through sheets of rain lashing against the sides of our vehicle and pouring over our windshield before we reached the Romanian border near Arad past afternoon. By now, Aruna had managed to wrangle an arrangement, despite resistance from the Bulgarians, that pushed the first game of the match to a day later than it was originally scheduled – 24 instead of 23 April. An extra day would have been ideal, but this was still a great boost.

In Romania, the roads, filled with canyon-sized potholes, weren't well marked, so we had no idea where we were. Once we'd crossed the border into the country, we switched to watching the *Lord of the Rings* trilogy. We moved quickly from *The Fellowship of the Rings* to *The Two Towers*, stopping at intervals to pick up tasteless and cheap food from gas stations or for toilet breaks in their stinking, inhospitable loos. We reached Calafat on the Bulgaria–Romania frontier and had another surprise in store – a ferry crossing. Bulgarian policemen stopped us, took away the passports of the non-European passengers – Aruna's, Surya's and mine – and disappeared into the inky night. Their ferocious dogs hung around just outside our van, so we stayed put inside. They returned after 20 minutes and uneventfully let us pass. We'd moved into the third and final part of the trilogy by now, but felt tired to the bone, sore from sitting in the bus and desperate to sink into our hotel beds. When we were close to Sofia, the police stopped us again, this time for overspeeding. One look at my passport, and the officer exclaimed, 'Ah, you're Vishy Anand? You're the guy we are searching for; please don't drive as fast as you play!'

At the end of over 40 hours on the road, we reached our hotel in Sofia past 5 a.m. on 20 April. The trilogy we had been watching was taking a thrilling turn at just 10 minutes to go to the end, so instead of jumping off the van and crashing in our beds, we asked the driver to take two leisurely rounds of the hotel, so we could wrap up the movie.

The time we'd lost ahead of the match could have easily thrown us off. Our original plan would have had us reaching Sofia on 15 April, a good nine days before the first game on 24 April, but here we were, battling sleep and dragging ourselves to our hotel rooms at the Hilton, Sofia, with just three days to go. It was a testimony to the spirit of the group that we'd stayed unaffected by the challenges of the commute. It wasn't a question of how much time we had. We had thought a week would have been ideal for us to settle in, and had been anxious about the pressure we would feel after a late arrival. But, really, the body will learn to swim no matter how deep an end it's thrown into. My team was quick to come around to this reality and did not raise a single complaint about starting work immediately. Our primary focus was on accepting that this wasn't how we'd wanted things to be, but it was what we had to work with.

For me, it was more of a continuum of having to broker peace with conditions skewed against me.

After my Bonn win, there was a measure of ambiguity over whom I would be defending my title against. In 2007, FIDE issued new rules regarding the qualifying events that would decide the challenger to the reigning World Champion. The winner of the World Cup, who turned out to be Kamsky, would play the 2006 World Championship finalist, Topalov. Bulgaria, FIDE claimed, offered the necessary financial guarantee to host our match and Aruna had a torrid time in the negotiations leading up to the signing of our contract. Some friends in the chess community even advised me to refuse the match if the terms were lopsided but I felt that the only person who would end up on the losing side in such a scenario would be me. I'd be dropped like a hot potato and FIDE would simply move on to the next guy.

♛

If we thought the road trip was all the surprises we were in for in this match, we were terribly wrong.

On 21 April, just as I was changing into formal clothes for the opening ceremony, Aruna's phone rang. At the time, the frequent use of mobile phones would inevitably irritate me, and so, every time the door closed behind me as I stepped out of the room, I could sense a whirlwind of activity within. This was the time when Aruna maniacally made the necessary calls to check if all the logistics were in place. If I hung around inside the room for too long, she would take her phone to the bathroom and finish the calls. The team and I had only chess to focus on, and Aruna took care of everything else down to the tiniest detail – from food to cough drops – so much so that my team members were spoilt rotten, reaching out to her for forgotten toiletries, a broken tooth or even a bruised finger.

But this call was anything but good news.

Our friend Frederic had got word of Topalov having access to a computer cluster with frighteningly superior hardware (we didn't know the exact specifics then) for his team to use during the match. Aruna chose not to pass on the disturbing information to me, and instead went over to the workroom and shared it with the team. Everyone was thrown off and there was some amount of panic over how this news should be treated. The crucial question they were faced with was how they would deliver it to me without upsetting my equilibrium. Eventually, they decided that they shouldn't keep it from me, and they slid this potential wrecking ball so calmly into our conversation and my mind that I was surprisingly not shaken by it at all.

Rumour had it that the said computer cluster was running the latest program of the chess engine Rybka and it was suddenly obvious to us why Rybka 4 had been held back from us in the run-up to this match. While we didn't know that Topalov's team had access to IBM's Blue Gene supercomputer (later his seconds said it wasn't working properly for standard chess software anyway), Rustam had read in a Rybka-cluster forum that it had a recent, high-profile customer. Now the pieces began to fall into place.

Since it wasn't us, it was clearly my opponent. It became clear to me why IM Vasik Rajlich, who'd designed Rybka and allowed us to use it in Bonn, had been ignoring my attempts to reach out to him ahead of this match. Rajlich's wife, Iweta, had assisted me during the Bonn match, checking lines for me on the engine and so was naturally privy to a lot of my analysis. I was worried whether it would be used against me now that Topalov had hired their services. Frederic, who was in touch with her, placated my fears and communicated her assurance to me that she would never do so.

We accepted that the most we could do was perhaps run our checks for much longer, but we couldn't be sure if the win itself had slipped beyond the horizon. The worst response to a tricky situation like this is to start doubting everything you have prepared, and, in doing so, allowing the computer to kill you even if it isn't doing anything special. No matter what you're up against, you have to give yourself some odds of success. If you've done the right preparation following the best methods, you have to go out there and believe in what you know. If you talk yourself out of everything, you're undermining the advantages you have right there.

Much like the ash cloud, this too was a situation beyond our control. There was nothing we could do to mitigate the strength of the opponents' access to superior hardware. It was decided that we'd keep this information at the back of our minds but pretend we never received it because it was like fighting a ghost. Unless we could visit Topalov's training camp, have a look at his computer cluster and test the equipment for ourselves, we would be constantly duelling with our own imagination of what it could do rather than what it actually did.

Once the initial wave of panic ebbed, we drew up a working plan. Our strategy was to play non-computer chess and always land the first surprise. Instead of preparation and tactics, I wanted spontaneity and flexibility to dictate my choices on the board. The hit-and-run method, where we use one idea, discard it and never go back to it again, looked like the most workable and pragmatic choice. We were stumbling in the dark with little idea about the strength of this monstrous machine that was supposedly at my opponent's disposal. As we now know it, it was us with 8-core computers against Topalov and his team's computer cluster with 112 cores.

But we too had help coming our way. Harvey Williamson and Mark Uniacke from the London-based chess program team HIARCS got in touch with us and expressed their interest in offering assistance. It threw open access to a powerful computer, which could now let us look into critical areas and offer practical solutions.

♛

The match began on an ominous note.

Ahead of it, no one shook hands or made eye contact with me and the air at the press conference could be cut through with a knife. It was bristling with hostility. Topalov announced that he would play by 'Sofia rules', or in complete silence. At no point would he speak to me, even for a draw offer. I remained impassive. There were other oppressive measures in place. Barring the urinal, cameras had been installed everywhere and jammers (the word was they were Mossad-tested) fixed at each corner of the venue. If I didn't ensure the toilet door was shut behind me, I could well be caught on the camera placed right outside the door as I went about my business. During the match, Topalov's manager, Silvio Danailov, occasionally paced about the stage with his mobile phone stuck to his ear, pretending he was on a call and was being passed on information, until the arbiter stopped him from doing so after the first couple of times. They were psychological ploys to unnerve me, though I found them to be more comical than provocative.

    I went into the first round feeling well prepared, but mixed up the move order on the Grünfeld. We'd been running into problems with it even during preparation and the solution we'd arrived at was shaky at best. On the eve of the game, Rustam had sat down with me and suggested a fix. Yet, at the board, my mind froze. I hadn't grasped the subtle details in this complex line and just couldn't find a way to reconstruct what he'd shown me. I could only recall Kf7 being a key move and in playing it too early, I lost instantly.

    I returned to the ashen faces of my team in the workroom. I could tell they were gutted. Among themselves, they were rummaging desperately for answers – was their methodology flawed? Should they have been coaching me differently? Would the result have been different had notes been shared and checked by all the members when Rustam was going over the line with me? I could sense that he was flogging himself mentally for the result even as he tried to lighten the mood with forced references to the British satirical film *Ali G Indahouse*.

Surprisingly, I was calm. I remember walking into the room and telling my team that Topalov's style did not allow him to defend, so the worst thing that could happen was that he would double his lead, not that he would shut me out so I wouldn't have my chances later. Topalov was the kind of player who locked himself in combat right away, rarely looking for safe options or the comfort of a draw. His belligerently aggressive style offered a crack of an opportunity for opponents. One could wager on him making a blunder and throwing away a spectacular position.

To take my mind off the loss, once I got back to my room, I binge-watched episodes of *Fawlty Towers* and *Yes Minister*, and endured a fitful night's sleep tossing about in bed.

I was yet to learn my lesson.

In the next game, I again muddled up the order of moves and got into a slightly worse position with White. It was now getting embarrassing for my team. Thankfully, I wasn't punished by Topalov for this blunder. Instead, he couldn't create any counter play, overreached and gifted me the point. It was wholly undeserved, I must confess, but at least, instead of no real compensation for a pawn, I got exactly the kind of trade-off the team was hoping for, and I managed to stabilize the situation. Coming just ahead of a rest day, it felt glorious. From opening disasters and hurtling towards a 2–0 deficit at the start, I'd salvaged the scenario. Suddenly, I was back in the match. Nielsen later told me that he and Rustam had briefly wondered if we were being 'hacked', since Topalov played in the exact areas we were weak in (though we had found new ideas to circumvent those shortly before the game). At some level, I suppose, they were also trying to tell themselves that if he was cheating we were going to lose anyway.

Back in the hotel, I was greeted with celebrations. For me, the outcome was really a stroke of luck, because by the time you get to the third or fourth game with a one-point deficit, you become conditioned to it and know that a loss may be imminent, but my being able to strike back right away essentially meant that we had just started a 10-game match.

For the third game, we didn't want to revisit the Grünfeld, since it was a sharp opening and the question of it being open to the analysis of Topalov's mythical computer kept circling in our heads. We were drawn to the solidity of Black in the so-called Elista Endgame variation. It was a great way to evade computer-powered preparation. The queens would be off quickly, which meant we'd have to wade neck-deep into strategic play. It was expected that I'd have slightly worse positions, but we'd analysed it thoroughly and incisively, and I knew that I could hold on to the game without much damage. We were headed for a quick draw, but since Topalov had sworn not to speak to me at any point during the match he was caught in a bit of an awkward situation. I was repeating moves, and after the third repetition, I could see that he was waiting for me to call a draw. I didn't. Instead, I just kept repeating moves while he grew more and more anxious. Left with no choice, he rose from his seat and went to fetch the chief arbiter, so that he could convey the draw offer. But by the time they reached the table, I'd made another move, so Topalov was forced to respond with a move too before the arbiter played interlocutor. I signed the scoresheet, handed it over to Topalov and neither of us shook hands. When asked later, Topalov's explanation was that he'd forgotten to shake hands with me. I was, of course, conflicted whether I should shake his or the arbiter's hands, so I did neither.

The interesting part in this match was that we had taken Kramnik's Catalan opening, which he had used extensively against Topalov during his 2006 win, and put it to use in games 2 and 4, and picked the Slav Defence, which he used with Black in his match, in game 3. It didn't go unnoticed. Kramnik got in touch with us after the game. With his characteristic deadpan humour, he told me, 'I was very amused you're playing like me; but you're doing it so badly, I thought I should help,' and offered himself as a remote member of our team.

My main Black opening started to run into trouble after Kramnik's association with us began, because he showed us exactly what was wrong in every line. Though I had four of the best seconds using decent hardware, his insights into the openings were phenomenal. I was amazed at how he managed to spot the slightest details that had simply eluded us. His understanding of the Elista ending was on an entirely different plane from ours. We had to plug a bunch of holes, so much so that we ended up losing any faith we'd had in the line. I remember Radek and Surya working close to 30 hours straight trying to rescue it before a game.

While Kramnik literally joined the team, getting down

and dirty, going over lines for hours at a stretch and pulling all-nighters, Kasparov also chipped in with Skype calls and notes. He had, in fact, got in touch with me before the match, offering help. I'd asked Nielsen to draw up a set of questions for him, and Kasparov got back to us with ideas and variations, even though some were slightly dated since he'd retired in 2005. As it turned out, he was expecting my support in the impending FIDE presidential elections, and perhaps he had reached out with the intent of it being transactional. However, it was clearly an extraordinary advantage to have two of the best players in the world with the most profound insights working on our side.

But that was not all. In the months leading up to the match, Carlsen sparred with me, as he had done before the matches in Mexico and Bonn. I felt I wanted to warm up so I invited him over and we played training games in the openings that I was hoping would be used in the match. This offered me both a strong sparring partner and the opportunity to familiarize myself with the material. Before Bonn, we played a tournament in Bilbao together, and he came over to stay at my place in Madrid for three days, which we spent sparring. Before the match in Sofia, he visited me after the Amber Tournament, and we trained for a couple of days in March, working on opening ideas and playing lots of blitz. He was the kind of player, even back then, who could play any position. It helped me test myself thoroughly. At the end of his stay, on the night before he was to leave, he broke into an uncharacteristic speech thanking me, expressing how much he'd enjoyed the sessions, and wishing me luck, before switching back to his usual self and saying, 'Or shall we just skip this crap.' We laughed and I said I didn't mind that. We joked that if he qualified for the next World Championship final against me, he should still come over and train me.

We may have had inferior machine support, but what we had on our side was a knowledgeable 'human cluster' that came together to prepare me and support my game. The eventual outcome of the match may not have been the same without it.

In the second half of the match, once the colours were reversed, I had two Whites in a row, which laid the what-to-play-with-Black conundrum to rest for a while. Eventually, I didn't get much out of the two consecutive Whites and was thrown into the deep end. With Black, we had been going into the games quite depressed because it seemed like we were running into nothing but problems. My team would manage to find a very convoluted solution to them and finally that too would collapse. It wasn't fun like it had been in Bonn. Here, we were miserable. The beautiful Elista was now making the team sick. We were fixated on defending a bad position, but having invested so much work in the variation, we couldn't just toss it away and forget about it. So we decided to go into one more game with it.

That my mind was fatigued was manifest in the eighth game. I came close to defending, but missed a chance to draw, blundered and lost. It's textbook behaviour that manifests when your mind is drained – you simply start fighting your own imagination and your brain begins to play strange tricks. In my head, Topalov's king came all around the board on the other side, and afterwards I couldn't explain to my seconds what my thought process had been at that point because it was obviously flawed. It was a sucker punch because I'd blown my lead and the match was now level at 4–4. Had I survived the game, I could have given up and moved on to another line with dignity, but switching lines because I'd lost is the least satisfying response.

I returned to the workroom after game 8 visibly upset, and my seconds attempted to veil their anguish and decided not to mention how I could have easily drawn the game. They felt it would only inflict further punishment on me. Among themselves, they agreed that pushing my luck with tough endings was bound to have this outcome at some point. I soon sat down for a short Skype call with Kasparov and, as the conversation unfolded, I could see my team members' faces turn pale, their eyes fill with horror. The cover that the team had so painstakingly tried to pull over my bad moves was blown off in minutes, with Kasparov explaining in great detail how I could have easily drawn the game. It's the kind of brutally honest person he's always been, so I should have seen it coming. In such situations, there's a dichotomy that you'll be battling. On the one hand, you really don't want to know what you could have done better, but on the other hand, you do. You want to know so that you can get closure.

I spent the rest day in some discomfort.

My lead had been wiped out and the scores ahead of the ninth game stood tied at 4–4. The team split their work, with Surya solely being tasked to focus on working on Kramnik's ideas in the Grünfeld, while the others toiled on the Nimzo-Indian line for the White game the next day. We had worked on it during our pre-match training camp at

Bad Soden, but we now had to bring it up to speed. Though the team discovered interesting ideas in the Nimzo-Indian, game 9 again ended up being a bit of a disappointment. I was meant to give Topalov some practical problems and he got into trouble because he didn't really feel the position very well. It was this back-and-forth that should have got me very close to winning, but the method of getting there was convoluted in its calculation. Similarly, he too came very close to escaping, but complete escape wasn't possible. For a while we were both on the precipice – but in the end I collapsed and stumbled into a drawn ending.

For the tenth game we decided to go back to the Grünfeld, since the Catalan had served its purpose and we couldn't refine it further. It was time to move on. Ahead of the game, Rustam came up to me with a piece of advice: I should let go, revert to my original style of playing fast and not overthink or obsess over finding the best move. Perhaps I took his words too literally, because I ended up playing slightly flippantly. If a move looked good, I would just play it and not hold myself back. Though I did get into some trouble, it wasn't the kind that could be easily pinpointed with White, so Topalov didn't really manage to hunt me down. In fact, a slightly worse position suddenly became a slightly better one, which suggested that my playing fast actually had an impact on his game. We drew game 10, hit snooze on our immediate problems and decided to experiment with the English Opening in game 11. Even though there were still two games to go, their value was so high that there was no way I could take undue risks. If I lost one game, I would be out of the match.

For the eleventh game, we switched again; this time it was the English Opening. What was happening here was that I was learning too many openings too quickly, so I wasn't quite able to appreciate their finer nuances. It's a lot like picking up a language in five days. From drifting towards an equal position on the board, I got myself into serious trouble and the clear danger of me losing reared its head. Luckily, that didn't happen and I even managed to mildly threaten Topalov before agreeing to a draw.

The immediate question that arose was what we should do for game 12: Repeat the choices that had made us suffer, or try something new? The team had to also mentally brace itself for the possibility of the match spilling into tie-breaks. We didn't want to return to the game 10 opening (the Grünfeld) with the supercomputer invading our thoughts. In the earlier instance, Topalov wasn't expecting it, but now that we'd used it once, we were sure he'd go over it and the computer would perhaps find a line that would counter it. If we wanted to make an impact, the surprise value had to be a lot greater.

My seconds craved for breaks from their cloistered existence in the top-floor suite at the Hilton, so we occasionally went out for walks in the park, which would also double up as team meetings. We did this before game 12 too, where I suggested playing the Queen's Gambit Declined. It was a solid opening all right, but I wasn't familiar with it and my experience in it was minimal. For the team, this was going to be a mad scramble. Much like in Bonn, I refrained from burdening them with the onus of having to take a call on the feasibility of the opening. Since we were to invest whatever little time we had working on it, I decided to risk it and assured them we'd play it no matter what. Kramnik worked alongside the team through the entire night and an English friend, Luke McShane, found a resource in the line early in the morning. He was then a promising junior player who'd collaborated with us during our camp in Bad Soden ahead of the match. The team decided it was good enough to execute. At 9 a.m., when I walked into the workroom, they told me that at 5 a.m. I didn't have an opening, but now I did, so I should just sit down, not ask any questions and listen to the brief.

My preparation went well, so did my opening, and my counter play was effective. At some point, a move repetition came up and he declined. It seemed strange to me because I didn't see how declining it gave him any advantage. I tried not to slip into the mode of waiting around for him to do something, so I started playing actively in the centre with the march of my pawns. This got his goat. For absolutely no reason that I could think of, he made two strange moves. Soon, I struck a pawn break. I knew that if he didn't react to it nothing much would happen, but if he took the pawn then I could tempt him with another one as well. To be fair to him, this rested on just one mistake in assessment. Had it been correct, his decision would have looked smart. He ended up playing fast, blundered and opened up the entry to his king instead.

It's what the heat of the battle can do to your mind.

Topalov's bigger error, which he admitted to later, was that since he felt I was better than him at rapid chess, he'd decided that his own best odds lay in the match not spilling into tie-breaks. That was a mistake. No matter what your odds are, you should never gamble too much. There's a difference between gambling and preparing to take a risk. What Topalov did on the board was a spur-of-the-moment act, which almost brought me to a winning position in three moves. Back in the hotel, my team, which had been working overnight and was ready to drop dead, watched me play the boring opening and was mildly relieved that they could now drift into peaceful sleep with a clear conscience and dreams of a possible drawn result. Rustam, however, couldn't catch a wink and came into the workroom groggy-eyed, only to find an excited Nielsen and news that he was least expecting.

I was winning.

When I realized it too, I tried not to jump for joy. I rose from my chair and walked to the players' lounge backstage. On the screen before me, I saw Topalov make his move so I walked back to the board to check the move for myself, went backstage again, sipped on my tea, allowed myself a smile and then returned to the board, and wrapped up the game, match and title.

Indian news channels were already reaching out to Surya on his phone over the development, unaware that he was asleep. Slowly, all the team members woke up to the news and ecstatic celebrations followed.

The effort you put into a winning match and a losing match is, in fact, exactly the same. But when you win you feel every bit of your work has paid off, and when you lose you feel you needn't have bothered putting in any effort at all. The results of this game for me may not have been as convincing as in Bonn, but it was expected that my opponent would base his preparations on that match, walk himself through the surprises I'd employed there and anticipate my moves more closely.

What worked most effectively for us was the team's ability and willingness to be flexible. They responded to the sudden turn of events – from a volcanic ash cloud and the disruption of travel plans to the rumours of the 'super' weapon in the opponent's hands – with minimum fuss and maximum practicality. None of these developments or events affected any of us gravely and we managed to find a good rhythm, an even mix of fatalism and positive energy, and just motored on with the things we could control. We had to switch directions quite violently a couple of times during the match, but that didn't throw off the team. They were even willing to explore wholly new terrain and see it through its implementation.

One of the hacks that always comes in handy during a match and keeps me from overthinking about situations or people is burying myself deeply in my daily routine. So even if an opponent is trying to unsettle me mentally it's hard to cut through my rhythms and get me perturbed. The act of focusing on routine doesn't leave your mind with much time to worry. The only time I really got to myself on a game day in Sofia was between 11 p.m. and midnight, and I made sure I spent it in the company of the blundering, hapless but well-meaning British minister Jim Hacker of *Yes Minister* fame rather than worrying about my opponent.

I also had a tiny revelation awaiting me.

Throughout the match, I'd noticed a tall, middle-aged man with ginger hair hanging around our team. He had a room in the same wing of the hotel as the rest of us, but I had no idea who he was. Occasionally, I'd noticed him poking around our rooms, looking behind curtains and shelves with a tiny flashlight. Aruna tried to put my doubts to bed by cobbling up an explanation about him serving as the cultural attaché of our team. It wasn't the most convincing story, but I didn't give it too much thought as I had a match to get on with. He was a helpful addition since he knew the delis and pizza joints around and had a local driving license, which came in handy when we needed to get around. He got us hooked on to BG Menu, a local takeaway service where we could order from any restaurant (like the Swiggys or Zomatos of today) and it saved us the effort of having to dress up, get to a restaurant and wait for the food. Only at the end of the match was it divulged to me that he'd been commissioned as an undercover security agent by Frederic to ensure that our rooms were free from bugs and cameras, since fears were running high of our opponents employing deviant methods to get the better of us.

By the end, I felt like the gun-toting, zinger-spouting hero from my favourite Terminator movie, mouthing, '*Hasta la vista, baby,*' with swagger and finality.

The story of this match, complete with imagined pyrotechnic effects, is the one I'd want to narrate to my grandkids. It would also make for a racy potboiler that would tell the world that chess players do a lot more than sit motionless, staring at moving pieces on a board.

I had survived the after-effects of a volcanic ash cloud, embarked on a 40-hour road trip across Europe, battled threats of a supercomputer, lived with a spy – and brought home a World Championship title. Now I'd seen everything. Or so I believed.

Veselin Topalov v. Viswanathan Anand (0–1)
(White) (Black)

Game 12, 2010 World Championship, Sofia
BLACK WINS

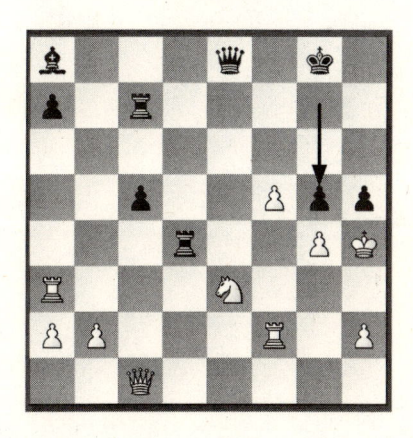

This was a match during which I was buffeted by the feeling that nothing was going as planned. In game 11, I came very close to losing and, at the point that the tension had peaked, my opponent suddenly cracked. This was the moment when the deadlock had broken, so there was a feeling of the situation finally resolving itself. The emotional turmoil of the match made the moment when I could finally see the tide turning in my favour very special.

♛

Resilience is the only answer to adversity. When tough situations arise – and they sometimes arrive like a hailstorm – your primary focus should be on accepting that although it is not the way you would want things to be, it is what you have to deal with, and then tackle it with practicality. It's also important to remember that no matter what you're up against, you have to give yourself some odds of success. Look deep for the resources that will pull you through – if you talk yourself out of everything, you're undermining the advantages you have on your side.

ELEVEN

TWO CITIES, ONE STATE

BATTLING LEARNED HELPLESSNESS

YOUR TIME AS THE WORLD CHAMPION IS UP, MY MIND BELLOWED. I zombie-walked into the workroom. My seconds looked up from their computers ghost-faced and we waited for someone to break the silence. My brain frantically ran through all the assurances I'd offered myself and my team two years ago after my loss to Topalov in game 1 during the World Championship match in Sofia. It wouldn't hurt to try that again, I thought. I cleared my throat and heard myself say that it wasn't the worst situation and I'd have plenty of chances ahead. But this time, my voice betrayed me. I didn't believe a word I'd spoken, and I knew my team could read the pangs of disappointment in them.

Gelfand, my opponent at the World Championship in Moscow in 2012, and a good friend, had suddenly taken away the warm, fuzzy feeling of equanimity I had felt after six consecutive draws, and left me to slurp on the cold gruel of banishment.

It was a fight to hold on to my title all right, but to my mind and Gelfand's, it had almost been like we didn't mind having a good spar and leaving it at that. Every day, through the course of the six drawn games, it appeared that we were just glad to sit across each other, play out our preparation, show improvements in some areas and take it back to training; almost as if homework was all we were there for. Neither of us put the other under any serious pressure. But this loss at the end of game 7 seemed like a breach of an imaginary agreement. It unsettled me. Suddenly, I was faced with a problem: I had to win a game.

It wasn't a new dilemma. I had been struggling for a while now to find a way to win. After my 2010 World Championship win in Sofia, I had finished second in Bilbao and Nanjing, tied for second place at the London Chess Classic, and the following year, in January 2011, got yet another second-place ending at Wijk aan Zee. To put it plainly, as the reigning World Champion, I hadn't won a single tournament in two years. There was some comfort since my rating wasn't gravely affected. I took a break from playing tournaments after my son, Akhil, was born in April 2011. I remember spending the night with Aruna in the hospital before Akhil was born, and I knew my life would never be the same again. I made earnest efforts to help with the baby. Truth be told, my job was limited to changing diapers and invariably finding myself sprayed upon. It was more often I who needed a change after that.

In July, Carlsen overtook me as World No. 1 and, somewhere in the midst of it all, I suddenly hit a wall in my game. I finished poorly in the Bilbao Masters in 2011, played out a string of nine draws at the Tal Memorial and had a disastrous outing at the London Chess Classic the same year. That was three awful results in as many months. After the first instance, I told myself that such things happen and can be fixed. But there was another tiny problem: It wasn't very obvious to me what I had to fix. I felt like a skydiver free-falling face down, with no promise of a parachute opening up to save him from a gruesome end.

I didn't have much time to dwell on it. I had a World Championship match to play in May 2012, and it was imperative I put my angst on hold and defend my title. What I hadn't anticipated then was that I'd run into a creative crisis. It would only get worse with time.

It wasn't as though this catastrophe had blown up in my face out of nowhere. I was playing World Championship matches every other year. At that point, I didn't want to continue thinking about what was going wrong with my winning percentage in other games through the year, so I'd drop the thought and focus on the match at hand. It was a mistake. I'd prepare for the match and win, but be right back where I started because the good result masked the problems in my game. It was easy to be deluded into thinking I'd finally hit my stride and could now go in for the climb. There was also an innate reluctance to work right after a World Championship, because the continuous play and tension makes you sick of work, sick of chess.

Through the entire second half of 2011, up until my match against Gelfand, I won just four classical games. Sometimes, terrible statistics stick in your head like an old song. My team sensed the crisis I was in when I began losing to Rustam in rapid training games at the three-month camp we started in mid-January 2012 in Bad Soden. It had never happened before. At the Bundesliga in April that year, I found myself in a nasty fix against Sergei Tiviakov and lost to him before going on to win against the German player Rainer Buhmann. Although the intermittent wins came along, clearly something was terribly wrong. Psychologically, I had turned into a porcupine. I was able to sit patiently and wait for a chance to present itself, since not winning games in a match is not a problem as long as you don't lose them either. But I just couldn't bring anything new or creative to the board.

The match against Gelfand in Moscow in May 2012 suddenly laid bare to the world everything that had been afflicting my game. When I look back on it now, it strikes me that I'd stopped growing as a chess player. A younger crop of players was coming up with a bunch of new ideas and I was slow off the blocks. It was the reason I couldn't put any of my opponents under sufficient pressure. As an opponent, Gelfand felt familiar. A year older than me, his approach to chess was similar to mine. In the classical format, Gelfand hadn't beaten me since 1993 and our ratings had diverged since. It should have been a relief – but, as it turned out, it wasn't.

The team had been together for a while now. It was our third match for the World Championship title in five years, and months of being locked up together had turned us into a jaded, vapid unit. Unlike in Bonn in 2008, when our work was fresh and brimming with novelty, this match felt like an obligation, a burden we wanted to offload. The work was still solid and polished, but the spark was missing. We just wanted to get done with the match, break free from our chained coexistence and scream into our pillows. We were, after all, five guys staying away from our families, wives and children, chomping on junk food and going for endless coffee refills for the greater part of five years now. In Moscow too, we were working round the clock and woke up to our sequestered existence when one day we came across a picture of a beautifully lit up Kremlin and St Basil's Cathedral that Eric, who was travelling with us, had posted on his blog. We parted the curtains and realized that the view was the one from our window. Before the match, though, we got around to establishing a moderately healthier routine, cutting down on coffee and making time for exercise. Surya helpfully lodged a giant Swiss exercise ball inside the training room. We caught a break on it between sessions, did our crunches and push-ups, and I managed to get some relief for my sore lower back. In my enthusiasm to give Akhil company at the play gym, I'd tried to balance myself on a bike meant for children below three years, fallen off and hurt my back quite badly. On 9 May, on the eve of the match, we had a bit of excitement as our room was unexpectedly invaded by armed security guards. We had apparently left a window open, which faced the Kremlin, where Russian President Vladimir Putin was addressing the World War II anniversary of the Soviet win over Germany, and a police boat patrolling along the Moskva River had noticed it and alerted the guards on the ground.

Anyhow, by the end of game 7, it was clear that Gelfand wasn't troubled or impressed by my opening choices. I hadn't managed to devise a single scheme to worry him. Our three-month training camp had revolved around building my Black repertoire. The idea was not to lose with Black and pick up whatever wins came our way with White. It was symptomatic of the passivity with which I viewed this match. I wanted to win because I was afraid to lose.

The defeat in game 7 bruised me severely. That night, I began to speak of myself in the past tense to Aruna, almost like a hermit who used to play chess in another life. It was one of my darkest moments. My team gave up trying to cheer me up pretty early on after that loss. They knew it never worked. Instead, they promised they'd have ideas with White for me before breakfast the next morning. I fitfully tossed around in bed and at 9.30 a.m. on the morning of game 8, I walked into the training area, and was met with a roomful of eyes that hadn't slept all night. I felt both inspired and guilty. I had to pull myself together. I owed it to my team. I didn't know how long I could keep up the intensity of this feeling, so a breakthrough had to come soon.

I went to the playing hall with the intent of putting up a fight. Though Gelfand didn't deviate from his big systems, he went for a different sideline and, pretty soon, I had to step away from any sort of work we had done during preparation. I played a quirky line, which led to a fresh challenge, and right away Gelfand was forced to think for himself. The game was now hitting an interesting bend and that was good news for me. It fed my urge to create positions to my taste. Imperceptible difficulties began appearing for Gelfand. I'd gained a bit of space and my king was comfortable, almost at a sprawl, and I was plotting my advance to the kingside.

The bear pit my opponent found himself in wasn't a total surprise. It was an example of a typical approach towards vexing scenarios. Faced with a minor problem when none is expected, one attempts to avoid it, but that only makes the situation worse. He had decided to calculate a long line. If it worked, it was bound to solve many of his worries.

Essentially, he was shifting the pivot. In telling himself that he was going to gamble on the long line working for him, he'd missed one tiny but elementary move. There were two queen moves I could make at the end of this combination. Funnily enough, the one I'd missed, Qf6, turned out to be the one Gelfand played. It dispatched me on a ruminative trip. I noticed Qf4, but the idea that he could escape Qg1 presented itself. His position wasn't very clear and something was swirling in my head, almost in a tumble-wash state. I thought at first that I would need to stall Qg1, and then, almost in a flash, it struck me that Qf2 instead of Qf4 would trap his queen completely, leaving him with no exit square. I felt my heart hammering against my ribs, my legs began to seize and my mind screamed, 'Oh my god! I'm going to win this game!' I gulped down the euphoria and held up an exterior of calm. 'Just a few minutes left… Don't botch this up… Remember the notes… When you're winning, go get some tea,' I repeated to myself on loop. By now Gelfand was waking up to the eventuality that awaited him. I went over the lines again, checking, rechecking and checking again. Then I played Qf2, rose to my feet and left the board. Gelfand sat there, thinking, for what seemed like an eternity. He resigned soon after I returned to the board.

I'd swum out of the undertow.

It was a lucky break, not a triumph of willpower or fighting spirit or the brilliance of a new idea. It was more a rare extra chance. A year later, I would learn that such chances don't come to you simply because you go looking for them. They're just about as common as sighting a snow leopard while on a morning run. But it was a free point all right, and I was happy to run away with it.

Suddenly, I'd landed exactly where I was after game 2 against Topalov in Sofia. The pressure stomping on my chest had been lifted right before a rest day. I could tell that Gelfand was kicking himself for blowing a massive opportunity. It was just the kind of opportunity I was jockeying for. It also meant we could both slightly modify our openings and go back to not getting each other under the pump.

As a team, we agreed that we were starved of inspiration and our match preparation had worked out really badly so far. When we struck upon the Rossolimo Variation of the Sicilian Defence as the surprise we could spring on Gelfand for the ninth game with Black, Rustam suggested, since no one on the team was an expert on the set-up, that we seek Adams's assistance. They'd collaborated in the past and Adams was more than willing to step in.

The match now began to stir to life. Gelfand's preparation was robust and deep, and we almost wished we'd played the match with this approach right from game 1. Three more draws later, we quickly hit the play-offs of four rapid games.

Each player is allowed visits to their team during breaks in the rapid games, and I chose Nielsen and Rustam to be lodged with their laptops backstage. Surya had shown me a lovely line – where the king does a walk in the open – and I was smitten by it. I asked my team not to work too deeply on it, in the belief that I could go ahead and play it. It's a helpful way of thinking, and also a mark of spirit to back yourself and play the chess you want to without having everything worked out in advance to the tiniest detail. A chess player is more than a professor reading out a lecture from his prepared notes. My positive rapid score gave the team hope, but we simply couldn't wish away the gnawing feeling that I might soon wind up as an 'ex-World Champion'.

Still, it was not the kind of deep despair I was battling after game 7. A tough first game in the rapid, where I went from winning at one point to losing my way to the demands of accurate calculation and finally ending in a draw, was again a signpost that I hated to see. It was proof that I was not playing well. I used Surya's idea in the second game, and Gelfand tried to put up a fight. It oscillated, and I had a feeling that the advantage was slipping away, but couldn't quite figure out what I needed to do. Instead of trying to draw, I tried to put him under pressure and play on his limited time.

This drew Kasparov's criticism and he observed that in his era he would have drawn that game. He had offered to assist Gelfand for the match, but the latter had turned him down. It was clear that Kasparov was available to anyone playing against me since our relations were strained over me not extending support publicly for his FIDE election pitch. I have to admit that while his comments against me were quite vehement at the time, they were not entirely unjustified. I agreed with many of his thoughts, which were valid, even though I couldn't say so publicly. This particular criticism about the tie-break, however, was absurd, I felt. In my view, you have to take your chances in a match and, if your opponent is low on time, you try to use that to your advantage. Essentially, you do what you have to do. Frankly, I have little doubt that the younger generation would do it without hesitation. It wouldn't occur to a Hikaru Nakamura or a Carlsen, for instance, to offer me a draw simply because we'd reached a position where it might seem to be the obvious choice. In this case, I'd persevered, and Gelfand had blundered into a lost rook endgame.

In the third game, I snuggled into a good position, blew it and waded into a lost one. It was one of those nervy games where you feel your capillaries could burst – I tried to drum up a counter play and swam out of trouble, only to jump right back into it. I just couldn't deal with the pressure. Gelfand too wanted to win this one badly. In the end, we reached a position where I could have made a fairly simple draw, but instead found a complex one, and it hit me that I had miscalculated and was now lost. I pulled a straight face over a completely flustered one and it seemed Gelfand had also blanked out. He was under the impression that it was headed for a draw and was looking for ways to avoid one. Clearly, we were both hallucinating and had the wrong position in our heads. It ended up being an easy draw for me. One that could just as easily have been a win for him had he advanced his king.

The fourth game was traumatic. Again, I made the mistake of playing for a draw. Passive play got me into trouble, which I somehow managed to crawl out of, then outplayed

Gelfand and landed in a drawn position where I could just repeat moves. He soon realized that it was a waste of time and congratulated me on retaining my title. I won that match because I won. I didn't do anything to deserve the win, and apparently he didn't do enough to not lose either.

The manic months had come to a close. I was swamped with congratulatory messages and we went for our customary celebratory dinner at an Indian restaurant. My team had given it their all, even though they were physically, mentally and creatively spent.

President Putin invited Gelfand and me to his official residence the morning after the match. We shared a ride and I was surprised by Gelfand's disarming warmth. We'd always been thick friends, but this soon after a match of such high stakes there are usually some embers still burning. I wondered if I'd be just as unaffected and cordial if I were in his place and realized that I may have struggled. Gelfand's attitude continues to be a testament to his being a thorough gentleman and an outstanding ambassador for the game. During our meeting, when Putin learnt that I had got my early chess lessons at the Tal Chess Club in Madras, he chuckled. 'Oh, so you're a problem we brought upon ourselves!' he said.

I was World Champion again, but I could no longer run away from the evident deterioration in my skills. It was now more than clear that the problem had gone from bad to worse. I hadn't really been resilient against Gelfand. I had just held on long enough to survive the match. Gelfand too was not in peak shape since the time he had qualified to play me. He had a brilliant year after the match, so clearly the timing was unfortunate. My fightback worked against Gelfand since our styles were similar and I was able to cope with his game. When a problem is manageable and you deal with it, you have an illusion of being strong. It was true that I had redeemed myself in the match, but the warning gongs were tolling loud and long.

I took a couple of months off, hoping to return in a tournament in June 2012. At the last minute, the event was cancelled. This worked against me because now I had to wait till October for the Bilbao tournament, trying to tug at the little motivation I had left. I finished an abysmal fifth in a six-player field at Bilbao, and fifth among nine players at the London Chess Classic, both of which Carlsen won. Yet again, I was back in the dark space. I felt like a fossil hastily reassembled from a tar pit – except I'd won a World Championship title in between.

I had to wait until February 2013 to know who my challenger in the next World Championship match would be. The nice thing about the match was that I didn't have to qualify to play it. If I had had to, I certainly would not have managed. By this time, though, it would be fair to say I would have had trouble with pretty much anyone I came up against – Kramnik, Carlsen or Aronian. I'd got away against Gelfand, who himself had qualified as the challenger in the 2012 match quite late, and since he was older than me, he wasn't able to do all the things that could have troubled me. His old-fashioned style was up against my old-fashioned style. Even if I wasn't doing novel, creative work, I was still able to play against that kind of player, and vice versa. Someone younger, I knew, would have troubled me no end. Could I have survived then? I don't know. In the end, it was a close race between Kramnik and Carlsen, and the latter came through. But even Kramnik, a player closer to my generation, who'd been sliding down the neck of the hourglass with me, was playing so creatively and beautifully that he would have been the odds-on favourite had he played against me that year.

What I was going through was essentially learned helplessness. It's the passive rut we find ourselves in, so that even when an opportunity presents itself that could change an adverse scenario, we simply cannot take it because we lack the motivation and belief in ourselves.

American psychologist Martin Seligman and his colleagues carried out research on classical conditioning, or the process by which an animal or a human being associates one thing with another. As a part of the experiment, Seligman would ring a bell and then give a dog a light shock. After a number of times, the dog began reacting to the shock even before it was administered it: As soon as it heard the bell, it reacted as though it had already been shocked. But then, something unexpected happened. Seligman put the dog into a large crate that was divided down the middle with a low fence. The floor on one side of the fence was electrified, while the other wasn't. The dog could see over the fence and jump over it if necessary. When Seligman put the dog on the electrified side and administered a light shock, he expected the dog to jump to the safer side. Instead, the dog lay down right there. It was as though it had learnt from the first part of the experiment that there was nothing it could do to avoid the shocks, so it gave up in the second part of the experiment. The psychologists also established that dogs who had previously been shocked did not try to escape them in a subsequent experiment. Seligman described their condition as 'learned helplessness', or the condition of not trying to get out of a negative situation because the past has taught you that you are helpless and you cannot navigate your way out. Afterwards, Seligman tried the second part of his experiment on dogs that had not been previously exposed to the classical conditioning part of the experiment. These dogs quickly jumped over the fence to escape the shocks. This told Seligman that the dogs who lay down and acted helpless had actually learnt that helplessness from the first part of his experiment.

In chess, a crisis of confidence feeds off a cycle of doubtful and bad results, until at the board you don't believe in yourself any more, begin hesitating over everything, stop taking risks altogether and take decisions that are not sound.

Around the time I played Carlsen at the 2013 World Championship, I was close to that situation. I was pretty confident I could draw a game against anyone, but I simply had no faith in my ability to beat an opponent. I feared I would overlook something or they would somehow get away with their moves and I wouldn't be able to counter them. You could perhaps get this feeling of learned helplessness when you're facing someone you've lost to 10 or 12 times. I've experienced it primarily with two players – Aronian and Nakamura, and also Carlsen to some degree. At some point, my scores against these players were getting ridiculous and the hope of catching up with them seemed forever lost. You can't turn a minus eight or minus six into 50 per cent right away. But my thought then was to wipe the slate clean and pretend nothing had happened. 'Well, I'll imagine I'm playing him for the first time tomorrow,' I'd tell myself. At the technical level, I could not do the same thing because I had to take into account everything that had worked for me in the past games and everything that hadn't. Against Nakamura, for instance, whenever I tried anything spontaneous at the board, it needed to be something I was really good at or I tended to do it badly. In a sense, even moves I came up with spontaneously needed some amount of previous preparation.

Some degree of visualization at the emotional level might reduce this feeling of hopelessness. For instance, in difficult times, some people like to focus on life events or situations that are pleasant. They think about winning, climbing on to a podium, picture themselves with a medal around their necks or holding up a trophy, and that makes them feel better. The method I tend to favour is imagining everything going disastrously for me. I think of the mistakes I could make and I try to think of what it will be like if I lose a match. I find that it calms me down when I imagine that I can engage in activities other than chess – bury myself in a book, peer at the star-studded sky through a powerful pair of binoculars that log on to iTelescope.net offering astro-imaging and access to telescopes across both the northern and the southern hemispheres – and life will go on. This kind of visualization, which looks at the bigger picture, has always helped me deal with my fears and hopes. In a sense, I try to diminish the importance of the scenario in order to avoid the stress of it turning out unfavourably for me. Maybe at the beginning of my career I found it more useful to think about winning because that was what I was not used to. Later, when I had the titles and the prospect of losing them was at hand, it was different.

The other aspect is training or technical visualization. Sitting at the board with my trainer, I visualize and think through different game situations as I ask myself whether I can save a particular position, or win another one. Then I make a few moves on the board just to see how I'm coping or do a little sparring with my trainer. If he tells me, 'You know, these three moves you made were horrible mistakes,' the shock wakes me up. Suddenly my thinking is more focused, and the adrenaline is gushing. It turns out to be quite a useful technique to get energized again.

To my mind, technical visualization is more important than emotional visualization. During training, imagine you're sitting at the board and playing a game, and tell yourself that you won't have any aid when you're actually out there and you'll also have your nerves to deal with. Just attempting to simulate the atmosphere (although it can rarely be done entirely) can sometimes uncover details that completely escaped you earlier, which you can then apply in your study material and practise. When you finally get it right, you get the feeling of having turned into a stronger player.

By this time, my team too had begun to disintegrate. Rustam wanted to leave since he felt the matches were taking too much out of his life; Nielsen wrote to me saying Carlsen had made him an offer and he wanted to switch teams. We came to an agreement that he wouldn't work on the Chennai match against me. Both Rustam and Nielsen had seen me through my biggest wins, and we shared a comfort, familiarity and understanding that was both special and rare, and I felt a slight pang at the successful team now breaking up. It was perhaps a good thing. All of us needed to rediscover the spark, and even if they hadn't left, I would have had to make a couple of changes to get some new members in and let go of old ones. I was glad it happened naturally.

In January 2013, well before the Candidates match, I sat myself down and counselled my mind to act. I had to shake off the inertia that had me sitting and waiting for a point to drop into my lap. I travelled to Wijk aan Zee ready for a battle and put in more time at the board. I again won four games – against Caruana, Aronian (one of the best games of my life), Loek van Wely and Erwin l'Ami – before my game in the last round, against Wang Hao, turned out to be a huge disappointment. In that last game, I thought I had an easy draw and relaxed early. It was an expensive mistake because there was still some life left in the positions and losing interest at that juncture can never lead to a good outcome. I assumed the game was over and a draw was at hand. Three bad moves later, I was suddenly in trouble. Losing the last game interrupted my psychological recovery. Had I not lost that game, I would have left the tournament in a glorious mood, felt good about myself at the board. I don't know if anything would have been different afterwards, but I would have at least come away feeling positive and that would have carried me some distance. It didn't happen.

The Grenke Chess Classic in Baden-Baden in February 2013 ended up being my first tournament win in five years since Linares in 2008. However, the Norway tournament that year ended up bringing my hopes of a revival to a screeching halt. Had I drawn the last round, I would have shared second place with Carlsen and Nakamura and been a much happier person in the remaining months. Instead, I lost again to Wang Hao, who had beaten me at Wijk aan Zee, and that too in an almost similar fashion. That year, the running joke was that I was 'Wang Haoed' yet again; I had begun to ease out too early. Both these games had a devastating effect on my confidence. I felt there was nothing I wasn't capable of – unfortunately in a totally negative sense. There was no position that I wasn't stupid enough to lose. By this time, Carlsen had qualified to play against me for the World Championship title. It was a scary thought, since playing dry positions is exactly what he excelled at. I remember imagining with horror that I would play a decent match but lose to him in the same silly way as I had done against Wang Hao.

My slump wasn't the only wrecking ball. As a compensatory offer for a missed chance at hosting my match against Gelfand, FIDE offered Chennai the first right to bid for the next World Championship. It's not that I hated the thought of playing on home ground, but I was already fighting my demons by then. If I was away, on my own, I could focus on doing what I had to do and not feel scrutinized. For this, of all matches, to land in my hometown when I was anything but confident of my game felt like a sucker punch. When I look back, I can say with a fair amount of certainty that no matter where that match was played, whether on the slopes of the Andes or on a frozen lake, I would have lost, but at the time, the spectre and weight of expectation coupled with my internal crisis weighed down on me heavily.

I was simply a shadow of the player I had been in 2008. It's a hard feeling to wake up to; nothing short of a living nightmare. If anything, Carlsen was at the other end of the spectrum. He was peaking. I was rated 70 points below him, and I was supposedly the reigning World Champion. Even as a sentence it sounded absurd. A disastrous result in the Tal Memorial in June that year, where I came in at a joint second from the bottom in a 10-man field, made matters worse. Four months before having to defend my title, it was terrible news.

That year was the first time that I chose to skip a holiday in the run-up to a World Championship match. Ahead of the Bonn game we'd visited Venice, before Sofia we'd gone to Rome, and in the period before the match against Gelfand in Moscow we'd spent time in the coastal cocoon of Kovalam in Kerala. The idea of planning a vacation ahead of a match was to deny the mind too much time to ruminate over what lay ahead; it let me immerse myself in a relaxing getaway and return for training refreshed, happy and eager to win. This time, I felt I couldn't afford the time or summon up the confidence to allow myself a break. I knew I was the player with the weaker run of form heading into the contest and I didn't want to compromise any part of my preparations. I felt I owed it to myself, the Indian chess world and everyone who was part of my journey in the sport.

By mid-2013, I'd begun working intensively with many fresh ideas. The problem wasn't my preparation (which was still outstanding), but my practical skills, which were on an unexplained downswing. The question was how I could bring all my work to bear against Carlsen, who had the ability to slither out of prepared lines even before you noticed it. He was fresh and resourceful. Not only was he very good in all kinds of positions, but he was also adept at avoiding the ones he didn't like and getting straight into his strong zone. It was not a problem that I alone faced, even with my bad form. No one else was getting around him easily either. The only hope for me was to somehow conjure up my form from Bonn, but even that seemed tenuous. I wasn't totally incapable of doing it, but Carlsen's wins were big. Besides, there was his technique. The problem I faced was that even if I were to get to these interesting positions in my preparation, how would I decoy him into entering them during a match?

For the match, I had as my team Radek, Leko and two Indian players, Sandipan Chanda and K. Sasikiran. They came up with great lines which were evidenced in my first six games against Carlsen. In hindsight, I suppose I was struggling to process the volume of information that was being generated. Though I'd had four seconds in the three earlier World Championship matches, Nielsen would streamline all the information that had to be passed on to me and would be the one to brief me. It worked better than having four people drowning each other out and flooding me with ideas.

Carlsen was nervous and out of sorts in the first game. I equalized easily and we agreed to a draw. He played a Caro-Kann opening in game 2, an unusual choice for him. I would have been overjoyed to play it, and, in fact, I hadn't expected it at all for exactly that reason. We had done some interesting work on it, but at that moment I couldn't recall the details. I decided that it would be safer for me to stay away from the main line and went for the sidelines instead. It fizzled out quickly, and with a draw I lost the initiative I had gained in game 1. My wait-and-watch strategy actually favoured Carlsen because of his style. I should have been the one pressing for the charge, rather than hanging around and allowing him to turn on the heat on any initiative I could have looked for.

Though game 3 was better, I took a slightly pessimistic view, not because I didn't know that I was better but because the position in the game didn't suit me, and the following game turned out to be the last time in the match I felt like I did anything reasonably commendable. I blundered in the opening and then was close to a loss, but managed to defend my position fantastically and eventually drew the game. A rest day came in right after that. It should have been the perfect chance for me to come back, pretend the first four games were done, and start over.

But Carlsen had his forces deployed. In game 5, he ducked an opening battle as soon as I'd made my initial moves. I wasn't calculating with accuracy and perhaps I underplayed my resources a bit too much and came within sniffing distance of a draw. Had I drawn that game, the match would have proceeded smoothly for me. But somehow the draw kept eluding me. I would come very close and suddenly it would seem out of reach – and at some point, at a rook-and-pawn ending, within three moves, it completely slipped away. It happened at blinding speed and after that Carlsen suddenly became confident. His body language changed. I think deep down I knew right then that it was over. The miracle that had happened against Gelfand would not happen against Carlsen, and I just couldn't see what else I could do. I had to resign.

In game 6, I ran into the same problem. I didn't have any plans against the Berlin Defence. There were no more Caro-Kanns on the way either and I kicked myself for throwing away the chance to counter that in game 2. I should have gone for broke then. From a drawn position I went on to lose game 6 as well. The post-game press conference was gruelling. A journalist asked me what I meant by 'trying to do my best' in the games ahead, and I had to sit through a mildly irritated but civil query over his English comprehension skills. I met the man a few years later in Doha, and both of us pretended not to have any memory of the incident.

I followed my instincts about coming back for a big battle in game 9. I didn't want to go down without a fight. My city had organized a phenomenal event and I felt a tremendous sense of responsibility towards at least putting up a respectable contest. For this game, I chose 1.d4 and Carlsen battled a near mating attack on the kingside with his passed pawn on the queenside. We waded into a deeply complex position and fluffing a defensive chance left me with no choice but to resign. Three points down, moving into game 10, I knew it was over. I'd had my chances. Had I succeeded in a couple of key moments, my position would have improved. Where I faltered, though, was in not having the accuracy to exploit the better positions when I found myself in them. I came close to improving my game, and then it meandered to the prospect of a slightly complicated draw. I rejected the drawn line, thinking I still stood a small chance. It was a fatal mistake, and, suddenly, I was the hapless prey. There's no way I could explain the three-point deficit. Carlsen was simply the better player. We played a fighting draw and broke off, with Carlsen jumping into the hotel pool fully clothed in celebration and me turning into bed early that night. Within a couple of months, he would peak close to a historical rating and start to outrank me by almost 100 points.

One of my major problems in the match was the tormenting feeling that the audience had come to see another player, a five-time World Champion, not me. It was embarrassing. At many levels, I felt helpless. After game 2 ended in a draw, I was already feeling hopeless. I wasn't ready to switch quickly from the preparation we had done – primarily in the wrong direction – and I couldn't find the positions I liked either. I decided that if I was going to try and land a big punch, it should be a well-prepared one, even if it were at the cost of running out of time, rather than a half-hearted attempt and going out three down. I chose to play solidly in game 7 and game 8. To many people, it may have appeared that I had already given up the match, since I was taking fairly short, fightless draws even though I was trailing by two points. As for the chances of success, I no longer cared about them. I just felt I had to do something. It was no fun being in such a pitiable state in my hometown. If I won a game, at least I would have had something to talk about, but here I was having to painfully sit through post-game press interactions, my blunders magnified on a screen before me and explanations being sought on my moments of brain fade. I tried to close my eyes and pretend all of it was happening to someone else. At the same time, I also saw a kind of justice in everything that came about. I had no one to blame but myself for where I'd landed.

Chess is constantly evolving, because those who play it are churning out new ways to approach old problems. The young crop of players was doing this remarkably well then. Being ready to fix your weaknesses whenever they come to light, and reacting hard and quick to problems that confront you, is key. This was not what was happening with me. I was so thoroughly invested in training for the World Championship matches that it was hard to summon up the mental energy to dwell on what to do differently, much less execute it. Moreover, the three title matches I'd played over the five-year stretch between Bonn and Moscow were against players who were roughly my age. What I'd missed out on in those years was coming up against young, inventive players, who would push me beyond my boundaries.

I was aware of the talk that suffused the match – that Carlsen intimidated me. It was something even Kramnik brought up with me before the match. What I didn't tell him was that it wasn't just Carlsen. I felt intimidated at the thought of playing almost anyone then.

Aruna and I checked out of the Hyatt Regency hotel in Chennai the morning after the game 10 draw had transformed my World Champion status into a thing of the past. We wanted to get as far away as we could from the familiar scent of the hotel lobby, its breakfast spread now imprinted in our muscle memory and the suite in which we had spent over three weeks. All of it was like sprays of mist which kept my disappointment fresh. I returned home to my two-year-old son's chubby feet and happy smile. It didn't matter to him that I was now a former World Champion. He didn't pontificate on how I could have averted disaster, and loved me just the same, even if I was the lousiest player in the whole world. It felt like I was breathing in mouthfuls of fresh mountain air.

That night I lay in bed, blinking into the darkness, listening to Akhil's soft snores. I could tell Aruna was awake on the other end of the bed.

'You know,' she spoke into the dark silence, 'no matter which title you lose, this, what we have here in this room, the three of us, will always remain.'

It was the first time in many weeks that I felt my face break into a smile.

Viswanathan Anand v. Boris Gelfand (1–0)
(White)　　　　　　　(Black)

Game 8, 2012 World Championship, Moscow
WHITE WINS

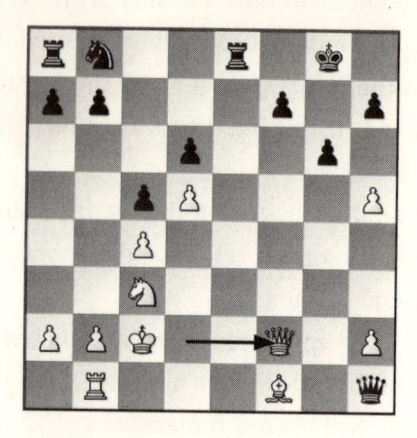

After losing the seventh game, my worry of falling behind in the match disappeared. It was already a reality. I just had to accept it. I felt I had lost my title too, and my approach shifted to just wanting to make Gelfand work hard for the remaining five games. The pay-off for my freshly acquired attitude came right away. In making the move on the board, Qf2, I exploited a blunder that Gelfand had made. I empathized with his situation, while at the same time being fully relieved at my own.

♛

Success can often lull you into believing in what is non-existent – that you have no chink in your armour; that your occasional wins make you invincible; that there is nothing for you to improve upon. Life does not raise red flags unprompted. Look for the cues – they will ask you to identify and work on your weaknesses, disallow passivity in your attitude, thought and preparation for success. Even when you hit the lowest point, they will offer a handy start to hitting the road to recovery.

TWELVE

STAYING ALIVE

ON TODAY'S WINS AND TOMORROW'S HORIZONS

I CAN'T RECALL THE FIRST TIME I FELT OLD.

There was no definitive moment that yanked at my thoughts and filled me with cold dread over the approach of another birthday. It helped that I had borne the cross of performance-related anxiety right from my teens. It was a state of mind that never left me, even when I was at the top of the rankings heap or plucking successive World Championship titles. The constant feeling that everyone and everything around me was in a state of churn, changing and evolving, made me wary of falling behind. Not the ague-inducing, obsessive kind of fear, but the sort that had me leaping out of bed in the dead of night, wide-eyed about an imagined breakthrough in a position that I couldn't get out of my head. I'd immediately turn on the computer and work feverishly on it. It's not as crazy as it sounds if chess is the overarching theme of your life.

When you're young, it's easy to ascribe a spate of poor results to nothing more than performance clefts. But as I progressed into my mid-forties, such explanations became implausible. The 'phase' of poor showings had dragged on for too long, with no climbs or crests in sight. The damning bit was that I struggled to remember details – it was almost like they'd fallen off my head like Jenga pieces. I'd never felt this kind of a lull before. It occurred to me for the first time that this could be something else, after all.

I hate to admit it, but when people around me talk endlessly about age and its effects, I subconsciously end up joining the dots when I think about myself. Typically, when I mess up against a younger player, my neural pathways literally light up, signalling, 'Look! We told you this has to do with your age.' I felt this like a stab during the World Championship match against Carlsen in Chennai in 2013.

After that match, I avoided the sports pages of newspapers like the plague. I had no wish to read the explanations that commentators had to offer for my loss, nor did I want to know about the earnest obituaries that declared that I was past my sell-by date. I stayed away from chess websites and cut off all links that would feed me information on the happenings in the chess world. I didn't know what Carlsen was up to after he defeated me. In fact, between late November 2013 and the end of January the following year, I didn't know what any chess player was doing. I didn't switch on a chess engine till sometime in February 2014. I knew Aronian had won at Wijk aan Zee in January that year, but I hadn't followed the games. Eventually, the results got so fascinating that I started casually rifling through them. I got the raw games and began watching them, but then I had a funny feeling that my name may just pop up somewhere in some context, so I aborted my plans and stayed the hell away.

I soon realized that the best way to find distance from the torturous feeling was by getting a change of air and diving into a tournament. At the crash-and-burn London Chess Classic less than a month after the match in Chennai, Kramnik made me see why skipping the Candidates tournament in Khanty-Mansiysk the following year was a lousy idea. My relationship with Kramnik had evolved vastly since we'd played each other in Bonn. Four months after that match, when we met again in the gym during the Amber Tournament, we just couldn't stop talking. He'd recently become a father then and clearly we'd both moved on from the Bonn match. His voluntary assistance during my 2010 World Championship game against Topalov cranked our friendship up a notch. There was no longer a pressing need to view each other as sworn rivals either, since young players with robust ratings were now dotting the chess ecosystem.

The logic he used to prise open my mind to the idea of competing at the tournament was simple: I'd already hit rock bottom and nothing I did now could make it worse. It was my chance to be in a tournament where I'd be left completely alone, free from any kind of pressure. It would just be me and my chess. I suppose I saw reason in what he was saying. I'd also come to understand that, in two years' time, I would probably not qualify for the Candidates again even if I wanted to play it. In life, we can't always pick our moments. Sometimes, it happens the other way around.

I didn't really bother with preparation for the Candidates and remained preoccupied with the consternation of having to face people if I played poorly again. But three rounds into the tournament, I was at peace. I'd beaten Aronian with White in the first round, Shakhriyar Mamedyarov with Black in the third, and I had a feeling it was going to be a beautiful tournament. My game in round 9 was the prettiest. I beat Topalov, while both Kramnik and Aronian lost their respective games to Karjakin and Mamedyarov.

My game against Karjakin in the thirteenth and penultimate round gave me a scare. Though I kept the game very close to equality, we walked into an ending where he had a bishop and a knight against my rook. We agreed to a draw after 91 moves, which won me the tournament with a round to spare and fetched me a rematch against Carlsen at the World Championship to be held in Sochi.

Former players and media had given me poor odds at the start of the tournament, which was hardly surprising given my form until then. In fact, I'd predicted last place for myself and had been thinking up ways to feel less miserable. But here I was, staring at another World Championship match in seven months' time. Just a few weeks ago, the thought may have been enough to asphyxiate me like a boa constrictor does its prey, but I'd managed by this time to cut loose from the swirling, sucking eddies of anguish and hopelessness.

I boarded the flight to Sochi for the 2014 World Championship with my expectations at a bare minimum. Before the match, it briefly looked like Karjakin would replace Carlsen by default, after the latter dithered on agreeing to play the match over apprehensions regarding the venue and financial arrangements. We got in touch with Rustam, who was working with Karjakin then, to know where his loyalties stood if such a match were to take place. He assured us that if Karjakin did turn out to be my opponent, he would excuse himself from being a part of the preparations for the match. We knew he was a man of his word. Eventually, Carlsen came around, signed the contract and our match was on.

The team that accompanied me to Sochi was a small one – Gajewski, Radek and Sasikiran. Gajewski had been working with Radek when we met and soon after the Khanty tournament he proposed that I hire him as a full-time second. I thought it was a good idea. We got along well and I saw in him a modern version of Ubilava. His ability to see things I missed was uncanny, which made him a perfect foil and trainer.

During the match, I went through the motions against a still-strong Carlsen and wasn't wholly crushed by a two-point defeat. I felt a measure of surprise and relief at my unexpected turnaround – I had gone from scraping up the willpower to throw myself into another World Championship cycle, to playing the Candidates, winning it against a stacked field and qualifying to compete for the big title. The recovery – from plumbing the depths of agony in November 2013 to feeling the ecstasy of a wholly unpredicted qualification in March 2014 – took less than five months.

Over the next three years, until December 2017, my results in rapid and blitz tournaments convinced me that I'd grown slower and dimmer. There was no reason to disprove that age lay at the heart of it, especially since I'd been a speed player all my life. When you want to pin down a reason for the inexplicable, it's easy to fall back on accepted and convenient worldly wisdom. Then, out of nowhere, almost as if it were a whisper of rejuvenation from the universe, I won the World Rapid Championship in 2017.

The horrendous aftertaste of my defeat in the London Chess Classic earlier in December was still ruining my palate. I'd suffered a quick collapse against Wesley So on my forty-eighth birthday, ditched the post-game chat and gone hunting for a suitcase-friendly Santa and Donner the reindeer set for Akhil. Earlier that year, in August, I'd finished at the bottom, at a joint eighth place alongside Kasparov and David Navara, at the St. Louis Rapid & Blitz event. I felt I'd had my fill of rapid events and chagrin for the year.

To get away from the apology of a year that had played out, I dived into everything my son wanted me to do with him – from binge-watching the *Madagascar* movies to eating cake shaped like a scene from the films to learning a host of *Madagascar*-related trivia from Akhil. I was yearning to take a break and we rustled up a plan for a family holiday in the backwaters of Kerala at the close of the year along with my close friends from Corsica, Leo Battesti and Nicole. But before we could pack our suitcases and cartwheel out of the city, an acquaintance at FIDE got in touch with me and suggested I give the tournament a shot. Aruna too was of the opinion that I should go, though she communicated that through the very Indian way of nodding her head and saying, '*Apidi enna thaan aagum*? What is the worst that can happen (if you go)?'

A few days later, I found myself sitting across Carlsen at the World Rapid Championship in Riyadh. It was round 9, my jaw was clenched and my brain was hollering at my hand to freeze. Carlsen had played 33.Nc5, assuming I would force a draw. I had no reason to think differently. It was a guaranteed draw, all right. Clearly, we were both seeing things that weren't on the board. I ran my eyes over the pieces, making sure that I was in for a draw either way, and decided it wouldn't hurt to run down the clock. Two minutes later, the possibility of a bishop f3 check hit me like a hurricane. I was winning. I looked up at Carlsen's face and could tell he'd spotted it too, and was possibly kicking himself for getting into this position. Sometimes when your hand wants to make the move and you can't take the tension any more, you end up playing the move even if your brain is trying to stop you. Between giving in to the temptation and allowing yourself to pause and think is the moment that decides whether the game will be a straight-out draw or a neat win.

Earlier, in my second-round game against Leko, I had mounted a brilliant attack on his king with White, and it lifted my spirits. I soon found myself in a three-way tie with Russians Vladimir Fedoseev and Ian Nepomniachtchi at 10.5 points, with six wins and nine draws. A 1.5–0.5 win over Fedoseev in a blitz tie-break turned a brilliant tournament into an extraordinary one. I was undefeated in 15 rapid games, plus two tie-breaks, and went from almost giving the tournament a miss to becoming the World Rapid Champion.

I wondered if it was all a dream – that tournament alone wiped out a poor year dotted with poorer results. My flight to Kerala to join Aruna and Akhil on the holiday I'd abandoned was at 4 a.m. I had to leave for the Riyadh airport at 1 a.m., change flights in two hours and board the connecting flight to Kochi. From the Kochi airport, the resort was a long car ride away. I was exhausted to the bone, mentally drained of all my reserves and was certain I'd sleep through the journey, but I found I was so euphoric that I could have just walked the distance. When I read about Tiger Woods breaking his 11-year drought at the Majors with his win at the Augusta Masters in April 2019, I could see the parallels with my win in Riyadh. It wasn't a prelude to greater wins or a larger redemption to come; it was as though our bodies had summoned themselves up for this one show.

When something like the 2014 Candidates in Khanty-Mansiysk or the 2017 World Rapid Championship in Riyadh happens, the afterglow remains for years. When I think about some of the games I played in those tournaments, I associate them with the heights of pleasure. Khanty-Mansiysk certainly wasn't easy, and neither was Riyadh. In both cases, I wasn't thinking of a win. All that was flashing in my mind was a bright beacon telling me that I shouldn't ruin it. When the eventual title is not on your to-do list, when all you're looking for is survival strategies, and then you land yourself a terrific win, you can't help but wonder why it felt improbable in the first place.

What I was careful not to do after my spectacular showing in Riyadh was to delude myself into believing that the losses at London hadn't happened. There'd been so many bad results that it made me caution myself that this one win should not make me lower my guard. Had I spent the whole year winning titles, and Riyadh had come on top of that, I would have been in a dangerous state of mind heading into a new year, finding it easy to be oblivious of the niggling problems all over again. As it were, the results before Riyadh stopped me from going down that path.

The 2018 Tata Steel Chess Tournament in Kolkata was similar. To be playing a tournament in an Indian city and spending time with my colleagues – more Indian colleagues than usual – was therapeutic. I often wish more matches were held at home, so they would feel unremarkable; it shouldn't feel this special. The spectators in Kolkata were really enthusiastic and that kind of atmosphere automatically inspires a good showing. For this tournament too, I'd decided not to think too much and just enjoy my game. Once again, it came down to one day – the day that made up for all the troughs of disappointment that year.

I increasingly feel that just as when I was younger and I couldn't imagine what life would be like when I would be older, I now seem to have little memory of what it felt like to be youthful and vastly more successful. In the end, I suppose, you remember the stories you want to remember.

Over the years, the space that chess takes up in my head has changed. Not through meticulous planning, but out of circumstance. There have been stages in my life when chess was all-consuming. Even today, when a position is fascinating, I just can't get it out of my head. It completely takes over, like a puzzle waiting to be solved. The part that has diminished greatly is how much and how often I think about chess. With changing priorities you realize you can't be as self-absorbed as you used to be. For instance, when I come back home, I can no longer work the way I used to. I can't shut myself up for hours because I have a son who wants to spend time with me. Since Aruna always travelled with me and later functioned as my manager, I never had to choose between spending time with her and playing chess. But with Akhil, it's different. I've asked myself if I want to see his childhood slide past me like a montage and I realize that when I spend time with him, it is just as much for myself as it is for him. So we both have our 'roteens' (in Akhil-speak) and our screen-time curfews.

My attitude towards winning and losing too has evolved. Earlier, success was the cog on which everything turned. In winning, now, the primary emotion is one of gratitude and I've also learnt not to fret over bad results. Worrying, I've come to realize, is just a dark, blind alley and I need to step out of it naturally. Again, even though the desire for the big wins and titles lingers, I'm no longer fixated on either. It doesn't mean I'm not pursuing success; just that the trappings and fetters don't matter any more. It's almost like a journey from obsession to freedom.

I've also become tolerant and forgiving of myself, and it's dawned on me that failure is a hopeless endeavour. If you're failing regularly by your own admission, then it's impossible to play the game. Over the years, and through different phases of my life and my sport, I've reworked and reassigned my goals, and carefully considered the things I can continue to chase and obsess about. It's no fun to admit it, but it's clear to me that I'm no longer, by quite a distance, a top-three player. Before I aspire for those kinds of results again, I'd have to see them becoming a reality quite regularly. An element of pragmatism and awareness of your current strengths is essential to stay afloat or it can lead to the depths of desperation. I've also increasingly noticed that the fluctuations in my results are quite extreme, or happen across painful, protracted stretches. I can have really ghastly results, then some more bad results and then, almost as if plucked out of thin air, a brilliant win. The pattern is almost repetitive. I've readjusted my view, therefore, to draw a sense of stability from the perspective of the bigger picture, rather than from individual events.

My typical response now to a long break or a run of bad results is to use them as a cue to learn something new, give myself a fresh impetus and explore uncharted areas. Generally, I try to look at my recent games and gauge how players around me have dealt with problems similar to ones that have afflicted me, and try to incorporate learnings from their games into my preparation. In this, I've learnt a lot from the younger crop of players.

Aronian has been an incredibly difficult opponent for me and I've picked up a few things from trying to deal with his style of playing. Equally, Carlsen and Caruana. When someone beats you, you have to acknowledge that he strongly believed in his position, while you did in yours. When that result repeats itself a couple of times, it is evident that there's something in your opponent's conceptual evaluation of positions that you're not getting. It's not that you're wrong, but that your opponent is more comfortable in his position and is able to play it better than you. Essentially, any player who poses a stylistic challenge and against whom you have difficult results will invariably force you to adapt and change. And the ability to do both is invaluable for growth and continuity.

I also tend to look closely at the narrow escapes I've had against players who haven't beaten me that often, and try to figure out what I could have done to plug those errors. Sometimes, I've noticed them doing well in areas I've never ventured into, and then studied those areas to pick up openings and negotiate lines that aren't part of my natural game. Such explorations have always offered me connections and answers. As in any sport, and in life, in chess too learning must be constant – not just new material, but fresh methods of learning too. If I have to name a single virtue that's carried me through my years of playing chess, it's curiosity. There has to be a willingness to learn things you're not good at or you thought you were not good at. The process will invariably involve a certain degree of unlearning, and the readiness to do that is extremely important. If your way of doing things isn't working, clinging to your conclusions is only going to hold you back. You have to get to the root of a snag in order to make a breakthrough, because it's possible that what you thought you knew is actually wrong. Unlearning is perhaps the hardest thing to do, but it must be done. Any knowledge, unless updated, becomes worthless.

At times, when chess has got frustrating and I've suffered a sustained run of bad results or have been caught in unfair situations or felt like a pariah, like the negotiations that took place in Prague in 2002 to unify a split chess world, I've been tempted by the thought of leaving the scene altogether – the sport, the tournaments and just about anything to do with playing chess. I have no doubt that every sportsperson goes through similar turmoil. It's perhaps inherent in successful sportspeople to fall under the illusion of being in control of what they do, but it's not healthy to assume that creative fulfilment can only come from being ranked No. 1. There comes a point when you realize that passion, not perfection, will carry you through. You need to have something that moves you, that you're passionate about and wouldn't mind engaging with all your life. And the root of the matter remains that I like playing chess. It's the warm, familiar feeling I circle back to every time.

In the 'Class of Old Boys' – Gelfand, Kramnik and me – Kramnik, youngest among us three, has been the first to sign up for a retired life. He tells me he's now busier than ever and doesn't find the time to miss chess. It makes me wonder whether I can manage to keep the game off my mind once I've joined him on the other side. The 'old-man jokes' we thrived on when we were young have come rolling back to us years later. Gelfand and I would laugh our heads off over them, till one day we looked at each other in horror and wondered what we'd do once we turned 30. Today, at 50, that joke too has aged. We're now in the sport for the joy of playing rather than the pursuit of a ranking; for running into greying buddies and players old enough to be our sons in tournament hallways or sitting across us with wizened faces; for telling the world we still love a good fight; and for the odd title that we luck out on, making our bellies churn, hearts smile and heads float.

When I look back, some of my most lavish honours, throughout my career, have come not from grand podiums but from the most unexpected quarters. The first time I felt moderately famous was at the Goodricke Tournament in Calcutta in 1992, when I was mobbed by autograph-hunting groupies. This was after I had ruled over a Soviet field of players to win the Reggio Emilia tournament in December 1991. Then came the storied instance immediately after I became a professional player. On a train journey to Kerala, a well-meaning gentleman sitting by me asked me what I did for a living. When I responded that I played chess, he smiled and offered that it wasn't a secure career. 'Not unless you are Viswanathan Anand,' he concluded. I listened and nodded sagely, and didn't confess to being the person he was referring to. It is a compliment I still hold dear.

On my return from my first World Championship title win in 2000, I found a Victorian-style horse-driven carriage waiting for me at the airport in Chennai to ferry me home. As we crossed the bridge over the Adyar River, through traffic that had come to a standstill, the driver of a public bus on the opposite side of the road swung open his door, leapt out, jumped over the divider and ran over to shake my hand. I was as taken aback as I was wary of the passengers of the bus being inconvenienced, but they had all risen to their feet, clapping and cheering. That standing ovation remains to this day one of my most prized moments. I've also experienced times of undeserved glory, particularly the occasion when I was mistaken for a film actor by an animated fan, who ran up to me to shake my hand and effusively gush over my performance in my previous movie, as I waited to pick up my luggage at the Chennai airport. I smiled and thanked him, and he skipped away happily, his day made. I was glad not to disappoint him. Aruna, standing beside me, wondered aloud why I hadn't asked which movie he was referring to – at least we'd know which actor the man had confused me with – and I laughed and replied, 'What kind of actor doesn't know his last movie?'

In 2015, I was surprised when a fan named Michael Rudenko, who works at the Minor Planet Center at the Smithsonian Astrophysical Observatory in Massachusetts, pitched my name for a planetary body. I had no idea that's all it took! '4538 Vishyanand' is essentially a minor planet or a celestial object that's neither a planet nor a comet that is located between the orbits of Jupiter and Mars, with temperatures hovering at around -200 degrees Centigrade. I feel quite thrilled that I can go to an html page and check where it's positioned at any time of the day, and I happily don't correct people when they call it a planet.

I'm now in a situation where I feel I can compete effectively. When I hold up the trajectory of my peers to mine, I see I've fared well. A majority of the top players today are half my age, yet we don't seem to run out of conversation. I'm enjoying each win that still comes my way, but am wary of planning too far ahead, because I don't want to drag on in the competitive areas of the sport beyond my time. I can't see myself as No. 50 or No. 75 in the world, just hanging around at open tournaments or trying to qualify. If I'm not happy with my chess and where it's going, I should have the courage to stop. Occasionally, I find myself keeping an eye out for the signs that will tell me that my time to step away has come, and I try to slip into the feel of what life will be like for me as a former player.

So far, I've had a fulfilling career, with five World Championship titles to my name and more than a clutch of unforgettable games. Growing up, I never had a mentor in the sport beyond the chess books I read and the blitz games I played. As an Indian, I didn't know what being a globally successful chess player meant because no one had walked down that road. Now, it's my time to offer players of promise in the country a chance to make their mark from my experiences and learning. From being the country's first Grandmaster to witnessing the count of those who've achieved the distinction now spilling over 64 squares to a fresh board is vastly gratifying. There's nothing more satisfying than the knowledge that I've played a tiny role in sparking an interest and growth in the sport in India. Occasionally, when young Grandmasters come over to discuss games, it allows me a peek into what my life ahead could look like. It's what I'd want to pursue in a more structured, regular and organized manner. To be of help to young players, I would keep myself caught up on all the changes happening in the chess world – I'd rather not sit around giving sermons on the way things were done in my time. Public speaking and my involvement with the not-for-profit organization Olympic Gold Quest (OGQ) that acts as a conduit of support to Olympic-hopefuls from India remain just as firmly planted in my plans ahead.

When I look at Akhil today, it's hard not to notice that he possesses some of my idiosyncrasies. Like me, he gave up tennis lessons early because he couldn't wrap his head around being asked to jog around the court rather than smack a ball across it, and he's confounded by the bloodied brawls that a football game between his peers can turn into. He'd rather pick up the ball and hand it over to anyone chasing him for it than be shoved around. His idea of leisure is solving puzzles and maths problems, just like me and chess books when I was young.

When he looks up at the medals and trophies that now rest in glass cases in our living room in Chennai, I want him to know that each has its own story of battle and perseverance. I've had a little boy's fantasy of a job and today I carry with me the whiff of my many travels and games, along with the most pleasurable memories and oddball mementos. Through playing my game the way I have, I've learnt that it doesn't matter if the world isn't on your side or is disbelieving of your worth. Sometimes the greatest truths are hidden in clichés. Find your path, learn, strive and don't fall out of love with it if the payoff keeps you waiting. Just keep the voice of your dream alive in your head and the will on a simmer in your heart.

Viswanathan Anand v. Peter Leko (1-0)
(White)   (Black)

Round 2, 2017 World Rapid Championship, Riyadh
WHITE WINS

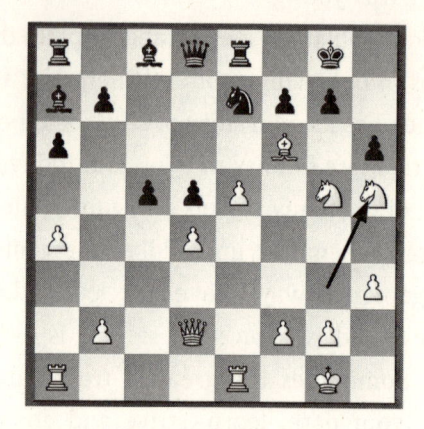

At this point, I had an uplifting feeling – not the kind that has blood gushing through your veins, but a sense of satisfaction. I'd offered a piece, but Black didn't take it. Then I offered another, and he didn't take that either. Then I made a third knight move. The board looked beautiful here. I would rather score a point than play a beautiful game, but when you can do both it becomes really special.

♛

In life, as in chess, learning must be constant – both new things and fresh ways of learning them. The process will invariably involve a certain degree of unlearning, and possessing the readiness to do that is utterly important. If your way of doing things isn't working, clinging to your conclusions is only going to hold you back. You have to get to the root of a snag in order to make a breakthrough, because it's possible that what you thought you knew isn't actually the way it is. Unlearning is perhaps the hardest thing to do, but it is a necessity if growth and success are your goals.

THIRTEEN

PAUSE, REBOOT

LEARNINGS FROM A PANDEMIC AND NEW BEGINNINGS

MARCH 2020. OUR LIVES WERE ABOUT TO CHANGE FOREVER.

I'd travelled to Germany in February for the Bundesliga tournament and, in the weeks between the games, hopped over to Warsaw for a fortnight's training session with Gajewski. We talked about how the COVID-19 pandemic seemed to be approaching us like a freight train, but neither of us imagined that it would bring the world as we knew it to a sudden halt.

When the pandemic eventually exploded upon the world, Bad Soden was a pleasant enough setting for a stranded existence. Flights were grounded, and the remainder of the Bundesliga was called off. I still had one thing to look forward to: returning home to Chennai in a week. That comforting thought had barely found room to settle in when India announced a nationwide lockdown. I heard the noise on the news, but didn't foresee its full impact. Though restless, I held my peace. At least I had something to wake up to every day as an online commentator for the

Candidates Tournament taking place in Yekaterinburg, Russia. It motored on as everything around us shut down. Commentary opportunities have usually arrived at interesting junctures in my career. Soon after I turned GM in 1988, I received an offer for the World Cup sponsored by the Society for Worldwide Interbank Financial Telecommunication (SWIFT). It was owned by Bessel Kok, a Dutch businessman and leading chess benefactor of the time. He had organized a few excellent tournaments in Brussels and I was asked to be co-commentator alongside Mikhail Tal. You can imagine the joy I felt as a teen at sharing space with my favourite player.

Back in Bad Soden, I didn't have an inkling of how bad things were about to get. When 20 March turned into 25 April, it appeared to be a temporary inconvenience rather than a lengthy ordeal. The weather in Bad Soden was lovely. I could go on walks and runs every day. Life didn't seem gravely affected.

The signs of an impending calamity made a staggered entry. The nearest supermarket, which I'd frequent for my daily groceries, was my window to the world. First, they began insisting on masks and then social distancing was enforced. Only 20 people were allowed at a time inside the cavernous store, while the rest had to queue outside for their turn. There were news reports of the collapse of healthcare systems in Italy and Spain and it soon became apparent that the problem was graver than I'd perceived. Back in India, things were hitting a bend for the worse. Panic and hospitalizations were mounting, lockdowns across states were being extended to buy time and scurry around to get resources in place. No one knew what lay in store.

While waiting to get back home to Chennai, I had the FIDE Chess.com-run Online Nations Cup in early May – a team competition featuring Russia, the USA, India, Europe, China and a Rest of the World side – to worry about. I was quite tense before the tournament and at the time it didn't fully strike me why. It occurred to me later that this was because for a whole month I hadn't studied or thought about chess in a professional sense. I was not in great competitive shape. It was as if I'd got off the treadmill and had to suddenly jump back on. I had spent the month of April relaxing, fulfilling my commentary duties for the Candidates and constantly calling airlines' offices to check on flights back home. Just before the tournament, I ran a brief revision and decided to plunge in, despite my reservations. Luckily the games turned out to be short enough. The timings were quite pleasant too. The matches would start in the afternoon and last around two hours. I would play two games and be done for the day. Every evening, I would feel relieved that it was over. The tournament went remarkably well for me. After it was over I wished I'd taken more chances on the board.

As days passed, it became increasingly clear that the only way for me to reach home was by booking myself on one of the Government of India-run Vande Bharat repatriation flights. I reached out to the Indian embassy, filled out forms and took the flight out of Frankfurt, bringing my three-month-long exile in Bad Soden to a close. The shock of watching a plane full of people in masks and face shields barely making eye contact with each other was unsettling. It resembled a dystopian snapshot from the aftermath of an alien invasion. I served half of the stipulated 14-day quarantine in a Bengaluru hotel and the remaining seven days at home in Chennai. It was a strange feeling to be cloistered in a room, separated from my family by a glass door. During mealtimes, they would knock and leave my food at the door. Thankfully, by the end of the week, I could wake Akhil up in the mornings and join Aruna and him at the dining table for meals.

Once I was home, a decision I promptly regretted was agreeing to play the Legends of Chess tournament run by chess24, which had players logging in from different parts of the world. I had considered withdrawing but kept putting it off until one day it was just too late. Truthfully, I found online tournaments tiresome, primarily due to the time difference. The games would usually start at eight in the evening and continue until midnight. I wasn't entirely comfortable with that sort of timing because it threw me hopelessly off my daily schedule. My performance in the tournament was disastrous. I finished ninth in the 10-player field, with a solitary win. The Online Olympiad that followed turned out to be uplifting as India finished a joint winner with Russia.

By the second half of 2020, over-the-board tournaments seemed to have disappeared. Honestly, I didn't find pushing pawns and rooks on my computer screen half as exciting as sitting across a living-breathing opponent. The pandemic put the brakes on sport of all forms and the world at large. My playing career froze. While it did the same for players everywhere, when you're past fifty it doesn't mean quite the same thing. In a way it was perfect since I didn't have to take the unpleasant decision of not playing tournaments. It was around this time that the dormant idea of my chess academy came to life. It was to be a dry run of what life could look like beyond my playing career.

In early 2019 I had been invited by the Bengaluru-based investment firm WestBridge Capital to deliver a talk for their employees. After the event, as I was leaving for the airport, Sandeep Singhal, the co-founder of WestBridge, asked me if I'd be interested in a chess collaboration of some sort. I promised I would think of an idea and write to him once I was back home in Chennai. It turned out to be the beginning of WestBridge Anand Chess Academy (WACA). One of the first thoughts that popped in my mind was the Botvinnik Chess School in Moscow and the defining role it played in the Soviet chess scene. A brainchild of former world champion Mikhail Botvinnik – the school helped raise a generation of players, famously Kasparov, Kramnik and Karpov, who later became world champions. A similar structure in India, where I could mentor and shape emerging players seemed like an appealing project. Initially, we had planned to get it off the ground in April 2020. But, what with the crisis brought on by the pandemic and me being stranded in Germany, it had to be put off for later.

During this time, online chess profited as an outlet. When it came to chess, playing online didn't require a forced introduction. As a sport, it had existed online well before the pandemic. People could log on to any chess-playing platform at any time and play endless games against human opponents from any part of the world. The accessible nature of the sport was an obvious advantage. The easy availability of instructional resources and the role chess content creators have played in the surge of newer audiences and number of online players has been significant. It's a sport that needs no equipment or physical training. A working internet connection suffices. The game is practically designed to be played sitting in one's room, cut off physically from the rest of the world. The Netflix drama *The Queen's Gambit*, based on the novel by American writer Walter Tevis, which dropped around this time, added an electrifying touch to the rising interest in the sport. Almost everyone I knew, even those who didn't play chess, had watched the show and were talking about it, and I could relate to it as a player. A superb piece of storytelling, it packaged the drama around chess games in a gripping fashion and accurately depicted the tension and exhilaration of tournaments. The cumulative impact of the show and the sport's presence across a variety of platforms, with some of the top players and streaming stars driving viewing numbers, birthed a boom. There's probably no right way to say this, but chess is perhaps the only mainstream sport that actually gained from a ruthless pandemic.

Even though I'd forayed into the online space through commentary gigs and tournaments at the start of the pandemic, my checklist of things to worry about before every online appearance remained largely unchanged. It included, among others, deciding where I wanted my webcam placed and worrying whether my external mic audio quality was good enough. Many top chess players took to this process quite wholeheartedly. They inhabited online streams for hours together. I never found myself fully immersed in that universe. I found a gulf between preparing as a professional and trying to keep up as an enthusiast. The two can hardly be compared. I hadn't encountered such a phase in my career before. A part of me began to wonder whether I'd be able to switch to tournament mode as seamlessly as I could earlier. Primarily since I'd stopped thinking in terms of fresh preparatory lines against opponents every other week. The process, despite decades of habit, began to feel slightly unfamiliar.

We had by this time hit December of 2020, but the situation worldwide hadn't budged. Physical tournaments and travel weren't yet on the horizon. It seemed like the perfect time to roll out WACA.

To WestBridge and myself, it was clear what the academy should set out to achieve: support and guide the huge pool of talented world-class Indian youngsters through their critical stage of development, fine-tune their targets and help them climb to the top. We discussed the gaps in the chess scene where our academy's intervention would be best put to use – primarily in the phase where players are looking to level up from being the brightest young GMs and IMs in the country to featuring among the world's best. It was an idea, if not a burning dream, that I had always carried in my head. I knew I would do it one day but had never got around to putting it together. The association with WestBridge for the academy was unplanned, almost serendipitous. I was chuffed at the stimulating prospect – to work with young minds, see the chess board through their eyes and gain a modern perspective on the game. There were other considerations too. Not only was it an opportunity to formalize my association with the friendly group of young players whom I would meet on occasion, but also, and above everything else, it was my chance to make a difference and give back to the sport. Finally, a long-nurtured wish was coming true.

By the time we formally launched in 2021, a couple of developments had come about – chess had gone big in the online space and, having been knocked about a bit, I wasn't sure at what stage my playing career really was. I didn't want to stop competing professionally, yet neither did I want to go around hunting for events to play. It was a sort of long, enforced break and I was enjoying it. The academy slid nicely into this space in my life.

I handpicked five of the most promising young names – Nihal Sarin, R. Praggnanandhaa, R. Vaishali, Raunak Sadhwani and D. Gukesh, and started the new year by designing training courses for them. We would meet online, play games, discuss suggestions, dive into analysis, and I'd pass on learnings from some of my fiercest losses and cherished wins. I invited three seconds who've worked with me – Artur Yusupov, Sandipan Chanda and Gajewski – to join as trainers in this enterprise of mentoring the next generation. The plan was that the young group would be periodically assessed on their progress and fellowships would be offered to new players every year.

Although I knew this was a temporary break from competitions, a part of me was already feeling like a retired player. I had no tournaments scheduled and didn't know when I'd be back traveling for them again. The opportunity finally presented itself in June 2021. I flew to Zagreb from Chennai close to a month ahead of the Croatia Grand Chess Tour Rapid & Blitz tournament. This was to allow myself time to quarantine and prepare to deal with any other surprises that could come my way. Part of the reason for travelling unusually early was to set aside a window for contingencies after a missed Grand Chess Tour (GCT) chance earlier in the year.

In May 2021 the GCT organizers got in touch with me after another player's withdrawal, asking me if I'd be interested. It would imply a confirmed spot in five events sprinkled over three months – the Superbet Chess Classic in Bucharest, the Paris Rapid & Blitz, the Croatia GCT Rapid & Blitz, the St. Louis Rapid & Blitz, and the Sinquefield Cup, also in St. Louis. It sounded insane because I literally had just two weeks until the start.

At the time, India was in the throes of a terrible second wave of the COVID-19 pandemic and the country was placed in the high-risk category by a majority of overseas nations. COVID-19 restrictions in Romania were extremely stringent and I didn't have enough time to plan a circuitous route through a third country to minimize my travel troubles. After the initial euphoria of being able to return to the board again, I realized that it was probably for the best that the Romania plan fell through. I wasn't sufficiently prepared to show up for a tournament at such short notice.

When the Croatia GCT came around, however, I got lucky with assistance in travelling to Zagreb. The Indian ambassador there, Raj Srivastav, turned out to be an old acquaintance who had previously served in Madrid. He gave me a call and assured help in every way he could. The organizers too pitched in with efforts locally. With everyone pulling together, getting there wasn't the most onerous task. I had hoped my early arrival would allow me sufficient time to crawl my way back into the competitive zone. It turned out to be harder than I'd imagined. When there's a game in a day or two, the brain just doubles down and does its work. But it's difficult to fake that urgency.

I spent the first week after my arrival in Zagreb isolating in my hotel room. I followed a lot of online chess events and played a bunch of online training games against my students at the academy. The relationship was symbiotic in a way, allowing me to benefit from their company. I also had some sparring sessions with Gelfand. After the quarantine was lifted, I could enjoy Zagreb a bit, though it got unbelievably hot. I went on wonderful dinners with friends, visited a few lovely lakes, watched a couple of football matches and attended an Indian embassy reception for the Indian Olympic shooting contingent who'd been training in Croatia. Finally, when my fellow participants began to arrive, and I bumped into them either at breakfast or in the lobby, the feeling of being at a competition slowly stirred to life.

Around a week before the start of the tournament, I had a panic attack. I felt I was not in any shape to actually play at the event. It was almost as if could recall nothing of what I'd prepared. I grew increasingly apprehensive about how badly the tournament would turn out for me. It wasn't that I was disconnected from the game – I'd been working with other players, watching innumerable games and commentating – but practical chess at a physical tournament somehow felt different. At the inaugural press conference, I tried to keep up the façade of the fierce competitor and a player ranked among the top 20 in the world, but deep down I wondered where I really stood.

The 10-player field would compete in nine rounds of rapid chess and 18 rounds of blitz. The rapid rounds turned out to be far from spectacular for me. I finished in seventh place with nine points from two wins and five drawn matches. In the blitz, I made amends, starting with four wins – including one against Kasparov, apart from three draws and two defeats. I could feel my confidence take flight. Outplaying Ukrainian Anton Korobov felt particularly sweet since there was a period a couple of years ago when he was a difficult opponent against whom I kept losing. I also beat Kasparov a second time in the blitz.

To end the event in sole second place behind Maxime Vachier-Lagrave was a mini victory. The result immediately placed me in an improved mental space to travel to Dortmund for an innovative 'no castling' format match against Kramnik. Castling – the king moving two squares on either side, and the rook moving alongside and securing him – is the only move in chess that allows for two pieces to be moved at one time, and it is also the only time the king can be moved by more than one square. The idea of exposing the king into the middle game through the 'no-castling' rule had been explored by team AlphaZero – the computer program developed by AI and research firm DeepMind – in association with Kramnik. Obviously, he came into the series of four games holding the edge in both experience and understanding.

Dortmund has always been among my favourite tournament venues and the weather then was just the way I liked it – cool and overcast. I won the first game, and eventually the match after the remaining three ended in draws, with Kramnik throwing in some inventive attacking play in our fourth and final encounter.

♛

Purely in chess terms there isn't much difference between playing online and over the board. For me, it's the emotional gap that's enormous. In Zagreb, for example, the hospitality was outstanding. Online chess can never replicate the experience of meeting friends, people who belong to my world, in person, particularly after a long hiatus. The nature of the virtual world gives people the ability to be anonymous and, from what I have seen and experienced, moral codes can disintegrate quickly. The proliferation of instances of cheating in online chess is one such by-product. It doesn't quite affect the upper echelons of the sport. In top tournaments, players are under enough scrutiny. At the casual level, as well as at the junior and sub-junior levels, however, it has turned into a chronic problem.

There are a couple of patterns to this phenomenon. First, people who are new to the game tend to assume that nobody has thought of cheating before. It's far from true. Chess has, in fact, been concerned about cheating for a long time – long before it became this easy. Security checks at major tournaments I've featured in have been quite extensive in order to rule out suspicion of participants sneaking in electronic devices. Second, if you're sitting at home without a video camera pointing at you, cheating may seem unbelievably simple to some, to the point of being alluring. From that vantage point, those distant from the game feel that since it's so easy to execute they must go through with it. Data, however, effortlessly spots such play inconsistent with participants' levels. Online chess platforms usually use algorithms to monitor how closely players' moves resemble those of chess engines. It helps detect anomalies and patterns of non-human decision-making.

As human beings, we aspire to live by a moral code. The obvious truth of it is that if we all follow the rules then everybody benefits. It's a classic case of co-operation. Often, people who behave with propriety in a regular scenario where they're known and being watched, act in a completely different manner in settings where they can get away with questionable behaviour. When two players engage in an online game, both enter into an imagined mutual agreement to play fair. If one cheats, the contract is broken and the whole experience is called into question.

The urge to cheat points to something deeper in human nature and the question of what binds us to adhere to moral codes. Do we comply with such codes only as long as we know we're being watched or when there's a threat of punishment? Take that away, and it gets stripped down to just our conscience standing between us and our urges. In this aspect my experience in an online charity Simul in 2020 was certainly quite educative. The event was, in essence, a bunch of successful people drawn from various fields participating in a Simul match with me in order to raise money for a worthy cause. None of my opponents were professional players and the exercise was designed to be a series of fun games. What was odd in my game against a young entrepreneur from this group who eventually emerged the winner was that too many of his moves were of an unnaturally high level. It was inconsistent with his status as an amateur. For someone who plays occasionally, his moves were too accurate, each reinforced by the next. After a pawn blunder at the start, his play was error-free. Truthfully, while I was surprised by his lack of struggle, I didn't instantly suspect that he was up to something un-sportsmanlike. He later publicly admitted to having used a chess engine for his win against me. A few of my other opponents too, it turned out, had played with assistance. It wasn't perhaps as glaring since they eventually lost their games against me. I presume there's bragging rights that come with getting the better of me or even playing well against me.

Returning to the question of morality, in order to cheat, you have to take a couple of deliberate steps that involve conscious choices. You have to set up the chess engine on another computer and follow the moves suggested by it. Whether you follow through with cheating moves or not, by such time that these elaborate arrangements are made, you've already crossed the moral Rubicon.

To stem this disturbing trend that plagues online chess in particular, I believe we should engage enough arbiters, add hurdles in the path of potential perpetrators and turn cheating into a costly proposition. The risk-reward ratio has to be altered so the chances of being busted and outed as a cheat far outweighs any potential rewards. When concerns over cheating had existed in earlier times, the scenario of a vast number of people playing online all the time didn't exist. Historically, with technological innovations, there exists a notion of lag – the time that culture and society take to catch up with such advancements and arrive at a consensus regarding their appropriate use, leading to a period of maladjustment or moral and ethical dilemmas.

In my opinion, how we choose to motivate ourselves, what we identify as the source of our self-esteem, and the means we find acceptable to reach our ends lies at the core of who we are. After all, values have a way of never going out of style – something Aruna and I try to teach Akhil every day.

♛

Much like everyone else, the pandemic threw me into the deep end of unstructured endless days with plenty of time to kill. Suddenly, I had nowhere to be. My playing career came to an unannounced pause. I could acquit myself of any feelings of guilt since I had no control over the situation. I was around my family, even if we were doing different things all day or were stuck on our respective gadgets. Knowing you're with loved ones during uncertain times can be comforting. They're the constants we want to hold on to, as everything else gets swirled and tossed around in a changing situation.

The pandemic presented us with two options: Mope about not knowing what lies ahead or find an opportunity in the unexpected gift of time. We had all the time in the world, with no flights to catch and no office rush to beat. I asked myself what I'd always wanted to learn but had put off for later.

Turns out, the answer was Hindi. I had never found the time earlier to learn the language. In my years of living in

Madrid, when I'd learnt Spanish by conversing with locals, I had never been embarrassed to make mistakes. With Hindi... well...it was different. My ignorance of the language meant I felt more lost in Delhi or Mumbai than I ever did perhaps even in Frankfurt (since I read, write and speak German reasonably fluently). I found it strange because I wasn't supposed to feel this way in my own country. It formed the premise of my motivation to take up Hindi lessons. I defined it as being able to survive an Indian airport.

My friend Anand Subramaniam, an Indian who lives in Chicago, volunteered to offer his services as my Hindi tutor. We met at the St. Louis Chess Club in 2019. He'd driven there for the chess event with his two sons. One of the few Indian faces in the gathering that time, he came up to me and requested if he could buy me a coffee at the café adjoining the club. We chatted and hit it off instantly. He turned out to be a friendly guy who loves his chess and a fellow Tamilian who had grown up in Mumbai. We exchanged email addresses and have since remained in touch. During the pandemic, Anand mentioned taking online Sanskrit lessons and suggested that I too consider it. I joked that Sanskrit was a faraway port since I was yet to pick up Hindi. He took the job upon himself and we began having regular classes over Skype once a week. Thereafter, it was him helping me with my Hindi and me fixing his chess.

The time difference left us with a tiny window in the morning on either Saturdays or Sundays for an hour of lessons. Among the exercises I did with him while I was in quarantine in Zagreb was to watch the Paris GCT event and attempt Hindi commentary. It turned out to be quite entertaining. In 2002, when my career had hit a low and I'd decided to work by myself in Bad Soden, I began learning German to give my mind something other than chess to think about. Almost two decades later, my Hindi lessons were playing a similar role.

I still think the best way to pick up a language is through conversation, like I did with Spanish, but my Hindi learning method was nicely structured and I could tell I'd arrived at a decent pit stop in my Hindi-speaking skills from my last fairly comfortable experience at an Indian airport. I could finally follow what was being spoken by the security staff! Of course, I'm still a long way off from being able to converse well in the language since I'm not exposed to enough daily interaction in it. I know I'll have to get a lot better at it before I bravely venture out with words rolling off my tongue. Now, I sometimes grab Surya and try and dabble in Hindi with him. It always manages to get a good laugh out of us.

The first steps of a new learning can sometimes be the most terrifying. The longer we put it off, though, the harder it can get to tick off the list in our heads. With Hindi I was determined to find a jumping off point – start taking lessons and make an effort. Even if I don't eventually get to be as chaste in my Hindi-speaking skills as I'd originally aspired to, I'll still be proud for not having passed up on the chance to make a start.

♛

Being back home and not travelling for nine months at a stretch meant that I had a lot more time to visit my father in

Besant Nagar. Unlike when I was travelling for tournaments, I could swing by the house at least once or twice a week to see him. He had a full-time medical attendant at home, who monitored his health and took care of him. At 92, my father's memory was sort of failing him and even though our conversations often went around in circles, I found it emotionally soothing to be able to see him often. He usually visited us on our birthdays and on Diwali for lunch or dinner every year and the running gag was that as soon as he was finished with his meal, he'd ask if the car had arrived for him. He just wanted to return home. I never quite understood why he wanted to leave so quickly. Perhaps, 30 years from now, I will be able to fully comprehend the urge.

In early April 2021, my father took ill. He was running a fever and complained of a lack of appetite. It appeared to be a bout of low-grade flu. He looked a bit frail when we met. I never imagined that it would be our final meeting. On the night of Akhil's birthday, 9 April, my father's test reports returned. It was a suspected case of pneumonia. On the doctor's advice, he was immediately admitted to the hospital. He had been a healthy man all his life with no serious issues even at his advanced age. For a few days his condition swung between okay and not-so-great. We could not visit him given the COVID-19 circumstances. Progressively, Aruna and I began to believe that the worst had passed. On 15 April we received a call from the doctor saying my father's pulse was dropping and efforts were on to revive him. Aruna grabbed some essentials and demanded we leave for the hospital right away. We were having a few gulps of coffee to prepare for a long day when the phone rang again. It was over. My father was gone. We hadn't managed to catch even one last living glimpse of him at the hospital. Aruna and I sat in silence, consumed by grief and guilt.

My father had been devout man all his life. He had been a stickler for following religious ceremonies, and we wanted to abide by his wishes in our final goodbye to him. He had made Aruna promise well before his death that no shortcuts would be taken in the ceremonies. We arranged for a priest and ensured his last rites were carried out in full measure. Later, I immersed his ashes in the sea. I returned home that evening feeling lighter.

Horror stories had been trickling in from different parts of the country – of hospitals not releasing bodies of the deceased to families, of people queuing up in choked crematoriums for unending hours, or having to hastily cremate or bury their loved ones at the unlikeliest of places. It was tragic to watch this unfold, especially when we'd come so close to experiencing it ourselves. Here I was, mourning my father's death while also trying to console myself that we had it better than many others around us. It's an odd thing to be relieved about when you've just lost a parent.

If my mother was my visible support system through my early years in chess, my father worked behind the scenes, making my life as a sportsperson easier. He would schedule his railway assignments and inspection tours so he could drop in at tournaments or pick me up from them. He had friends and contacts in almost every city and could easily arrange for my travel between tournament venues. It was because of him that I could compete with comfort.

For my first world sub-juniors in 1984, my parents accompanied me to France. I was staying at the tournament village and they put up at the home of a friend who worked at the Indian embassy. They would come to watch me play at the venue and take the train or bus back to the friend's place after every game. One day, after I complained I was feeling particularly drowsy, my father pulled back my eyelids, inspected my eyes for a while and declared I had jaundice. Then began the grand expedition to conceal this fact from everyone in the tournament so I could continue in the competition. His advice for me was to look up, down or away during games – anywhere but directly into my opponent's eyes – so my yellow eyes wouldn't give me away. I did just that and got through the remaining games.

My parents were also around to offer me support during the 1986 National Championships at the Rashtriya Chemicals and Fertilizers (RCF) complex in what was then Bombay. I was staying alone at the guesthouse inside the premises and they visited me to see if I was doing all right. There was a persistent if not intolerable stink of chlorine in the facility. I have often wondered if they fainted on their car ride back. After my win, my father had a car pick me up and take me to the Western Railway headquarters at the Churchgate station. He had organized a celebratory meal for us there. My brother was present too and it felt like a happy family reunion. The following year, he came along with me for the National Championships in Tumkur since my mother was away in America for my nephew's birth.

I started the tournament badly and, even though I obviously cared about it, I tried to act flippant and casual about the whole affair. Sensing that it could be a signal of his son growing wayward, my father decided to be stern. He gave me a tough talk about the importance of playing well to prove my mettle. At one point, Manuel Aaron, who was also participating in the tournament, politely advised my father that pressure tactics might not be the best idea to motivate me. My father waited until rest day to take me to Bangalore and make amends with tall glasses filled to the brim with scoops of mango ice cream. All along he genuinely wanted to encourage me but he hadn't been around enough tournaments as my mother, to know the right way to do it. After we returned, I went on a winning streak and ended up finishing on top.

In my early years as a chess player, my father doubled up as my manager and had to deal with a youngster who was trying to break free and discover himself. He was patient with me even in the times I would muck up the rules. Occasionally, I would spot my mother whispering in his ear that he should cut me some slack and let me do my own thing. My father would liaise with sponsors and accompany me for ad shoots. He would even offer unsolicited advice to ad producers on how they should go about their business. We once travelled together to Bombay for an ad shoot and I recall us bickering on the way. He was still getting used to me wanting to be my own person. Now, when I look back, I feel bad for having those fights even though I know they were perhaps inevitable at my age.

As he advanced in years and trundled into his late 80s, every time I was about to travel, my father would ask me if I was headed to Linares. I didn't have the heart to tell him that the tournament had been long shut down. In his final years, I've lost count of how many times he asked me if I had retired. He would lament over finding no mention of me in the morning's papers – a supposed indicator of me having been long retired. 'Oh, you're still playing,' he would wonder aloud in astonishment. I would reply, 'Yes, Appa, I probably should retire but I'm still not quite there yet.' At times he would suddenly jump up and mention a chess prodigy he'd heard of and I'd inform him that the player was a talent from two decades ago. Stories from his years in the railways worked his memory the best I realized, so I'd often cajole him into narrating them. What I could relate to in his stories from my own experiences was how travelling to different countries was each memorable in its own way – unlike today, when you visit Asia, Africa, South Africa and have the same Starbucks coupon to cash in and the travel experience has been flattened to a large extent.

Reminiscing about African adventures always lit up my father's eyes and he would animatedly talk about his trips to Zambia and Kenya on behalf of the Indian Coach Factory to negotiate wagon and locomotive deals. He would mention how the Japanese outgunned him by trooping in with their embassy officials and employing pressure tactics. All my father would tell his prospective clients was that even though the brand he was selling wasn't as fancy as that of the Japanese, it was of sturdy build and would offer them their money's worth; the needs of Zambia or Kenya were similar to India's, not Japan's, he would remind them. Aruna and I would often laugh over how my father's Africa tales almost always featured an episode of a plane engine developing a snag in a place other than the destination and the mishap eventually leading to the expeditions.

In his last years, my father's Sunday afternoons were spent in the company of his grandson over ice cream scoops. Every Sunday we would buy ice creams and take them over to my father's house. He would enjoy watching Akhil greedily grab spoonfuls from all of us. They adored each other and it was special to watch that bond from a distance. My father lived a full life and spent ten years of it watching Akhil grow up. But to me his final days will be inextricably linked with the circumstances the pandemic brought about, which didn't allow us even one final visit before he left us. Though I rarely demonstrate it, the pain of his absence feels like a giant boulder bearing down on my chest.

♛

When I look back at the worst days of the pandemic, I realize the learnings have been plenty. I've been forced to cope with the loss of a parent and that has drawn me closer to my family. When I peep into Akhil's room I see a child trying harder than the rest of us to accept the reality of online classes and his friends being turned into tiny picture panels on a screen. When I'm away, more than ever before, I think about home and worry if Akhil remembered to show his science experiment in class. I catch the proud smile on his face when my achievements appear as questions in his school assignments.

My approach towards the pandemic was to not fight the outlandish situation kicking and screaming, but to flow with the current without overthinking and making myself miserable. None of us could have been better or worse prepared for what we were up against. The one lesson that I have extrapolated from my life as a chess player is to keep up some of my regular habits no matter how topsy-turvy everything becomes around me. Foremost among these for me has been regular exercise. Following one or more constructive habits as constants works as a log you can use to stay afloat while everything else drowns in anarchy. Even if it's something seemingly mundane like making your bed every morning. It can give you a semblance of control and normalcy.

The COVID-19 pandemic came at an unusual crossroads in my life and career. I had a reasonable calendar ready, and even if I wasn't exactly on the verge of retirement I could spot it on the horizon. After the forced break, it was exciting and challenging to be able to play tournaments again. It was a relief to finally address the fear that I might not be able to play again. The feeling of a complete return to the board the way it was, though, is still missing. The long gaps between tournaments continue to feel unnatural. What do you do when the way the planet works is no longer the same? For most of us, the pause over which we had no control was about learning and unlearning. If anything, it taught us that it doesn't end with changing working methods and beliefs. For me, playing coach to a group of exceptionally talented young players was an act of learning and unlearning in every session. As a teacher I want to pass on my knowledge. But there's also a struggle sometimes to explain the intuitive decisions I took over the board as a player. There's no guarantee that a strong player will make for a half-decent teacher. After my first few sessions, I realized I had to consciously prepare for the role. I began to put together material in advance, anticipate probable questions and build the ones I faced in the last session into a lesson.

Playing mentor is slowly taking the place of a full calendar of tournaments marked for travel. The pandemic has taught us the art of substitution – being at home around family replaced spending time with friends socially, and my love for chess has taken a fresh turn. I wake up every day thinking how I can be a better teacher than I was in the previous class. It has supplanted tense games and troublesome opponents that raced in my mind in earlier years. The unannounced pause has also lent us perspective to look closely at the things we've been chasing all our lives. To weigh whether they matter enough to be ranked ahead of other aspects that we've perhaps overlooked. The blinkers are finally off.

The world as we knew it no longer exists. The things we took for granted, thinking they'd last forever, have long disappeared. The only rule now is to be aware of changing realities, let go of rigid ideas, and find joy in the new and the unknown.

ACKNOWLEDGEMENTS

Gratitude seems like a small word to describe what I feel towards most people mentioned here.

My parents, without whom I would never have been able to give myself to chess so freely. My father, for always telling me to be myself and play fast if that's what felt good. My mother, for waiting patiently for my phone call after every tournament just to hear my voice.

My siblings, for putting up with the fact that I was always the pampered and preferred one.

Aruna, for being my punching bag par excellence and for holding me up in my darkest moments.

Akhil, for showing me every day that fatherhood is by far the most exhilarating experience I will ever have.

My friends, Hans-Walter Schmitt, for sharing my taste in music, especially Queen, but more than that for being the one person I know who would take a bullet for me; Frederic, for taking me into his home time and again and helping me deal with technology; Albert, for being there for the longest time and for the moments shared at his home between tournaments.

Maurice and Nieves, for being my 'other' parents – their love and laughter will always stay with me.

My seconds, for working tirelessly by my side and for dealing with my chess and me.

Ubilava, Ubi, my first official second, for teaching me so much about preparation, and for his company that's always filled with mirth and entertainment.

Peter Heine Nielsen, PH, for giving me massive boosts of confidence and accurately evaluating my choices even after I had made the right decision.

Radoslaw Wojtaszek, Radek, my chess protégé, for being there right through my World Championship journey.

Grzegorz Gajewski, for the endless hours of work he puts in just so that I can relax at the board.

Surya Sekhar Ganguly and Sandipan Chanda, both of whom brought creativity and hard work to the table and stood by me always.

Rajendra Pawar, Raji, with whom my association goes beyond the NIIT connect, for making me feel like a part of his family and celebrating my victories in the most spectacular fashion.

P.R. Venketrama Raja, Shankar, for supporting me in 1991, when I needed help the most, and seeing in me a promise when most others didn't. Over the years, he has become a friend, a support and moreover a great mentor for chess.

My fans, for always being kind to me and for constant encouragement that has kept me going through tough challenges.

For Susan Ninan and Poulomi Chatterjee, a special thank you, for their untiring work in collecting and collating material for the book and doing an excellent job of telling my story in my words. The many hours they spent with me helped me relive pleasurable memories.

In 1985, when both my talent and my barely there moustache made their presence felt.

Friend, teacher and ally, my mother moved pieces across the board with me and would always be around to watch me play. Time away from chess was spent in the company of the Bee Gees.

A delighted 10-year-old after winning the *Chess Today* puzzle in Manila in 1979. Afterwards, they invited me to ransack their library and take all the chess books I wanted.

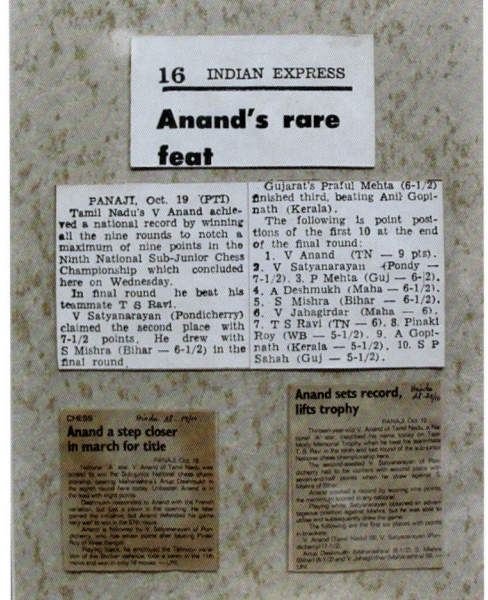

Turns out my aunt's sumptuous vegetable au gratin and the title of national sub-junior champion weren't the only things the 1983 tournament in Panaji had to offer. With that win, I also hit the news headlines for the first time.

With my mother outside the tournament venue in Panaji.

At the 1986 Dubai Olympiad with the England v. Poland games playing out in the background.

With well-wishers in Calicut, Kerala, who had gathered to greet me after my Junior World Championship win in 1987. A gentleman I met on the train journey there had innocently pointed out the vagaries of pursuing a career in chess 'unless you are Viswanathan Anand'. I didn't tell him my name.

Snippets from my earliest post-game notes. It's a habit my mother inculcated in me and one that I still maintain today, even if in its abridged version.

With a tournament official, Gyula Sax and Predrag Nikolić (l-r) at the 1989 Hoogovens tournament. Together with Zoltán Ribli, we finished in a four-way tie for first place with scores of 7.5/13.

Playing Alexey Dreev in the 1991 Candidates quarter-finals in Madras, a match I won with a magnificent 4.5–1.5 scoreline.

At the 1992 Melody Amber tournament during a game against Lev Polougaevski. The annual tournament which ran till 2011 had me winning the rapid title a record nine times.

Meeting President R. Venkataraman at the Rashtrapati Bhavan in New Delhi in 1988.

In attendance to receive the Soviet Land Nehru Awards at a ceremony in New Delhi in 1990.

Working with the Atari in 1989 at the home of ChessBase co-founder and my dear friend Frederic Friedel in Hamburg. His young son Thomas looks on.

A rousing welcome at Gorky Sadan in Calcutta in 1992. My Reggio Emilia win in December 1991, which saw me finishing ahead of Kasparov and Karpov, had catapulted me to mini-stardom.

With legendary film-maker and doyen of Indian cinema Satyajit Ray in Calcutta in 1992.

At home in Collado Mediano with my team of seconds in full attendance ahead of the 1995 World Championship match against Kasparov in New York.

During the 1995 match against Kasparov. I had a handy what-not-to-do-in-a-match list by the end of it.

According to Aruna, my request for a second cup of coffee when I visited her home for the first time had her mother pulling her to the kitchen and saying, 'You have to marry him!' We did, in June 1996.

With Aruna, during the 'honeymoon chess tournament' in Dortmund in 1996.

With Kramnik (second from left) and my friend Hans-Walter Schmitt (extreme right) at the 1996 Dortmund tournament. After every game, Aruna would rush out of the playing hall and wait in the ladies' restroom until I strolled over, called out to her and told her the result. She was still new to the chess scene and couldn't always tell if I'd won or lost a game.

My first tournament after marriage in Dortmund, in July 1996, turned out to be a spectacular one. I tied for first place with Kramnik and finished a full point ahead of the rest of the field.

With my trainer Elizbar Ubilava, who brought unconventional chess positions and Georgian food into my life. The Georgian traditional cheese bread, Khacchapuri, remains an enduring favourite.

An old Russian joke always cracked us up. A man was playing chess on the beach with his dog, and a crowd gathered in wonderment and gushed, 'How remarkable!' The man angrily protested, 'What's so remarkable? I'm leading three games to one!' It's a story that would before long be true of chess players and computers.

Catching a break with Kramnik at the Monte Carlo Open in Monaco in 1997.

With (l-r) John Nunn, Predrag Nikolić, my friend Ram Bhatt and Joël Lautier at the Amber Tournament in Monaco in 1996.

Always a novelty to look forward to – deciding the playing sequence through a remote-controlled car race alongside Topalov and Jeroen Piket at the Amber Tournament in Monaco in 1996–97.

I got to be Top Gun at the opening ceremony of the Amber Tournament in Monaco in 1999!

Playing Karpov at the FIDE World Championship in Laussane in 1998.

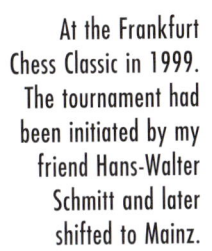

At the Frankfurt Chess Classic in 1999. The tournament had been initiated by my friend Hans-Walter Schmitt and later shifted to Mainz.

At the Chess Classic in Mainz in 2002. The splendid annual rapid tournament ran from 2001 to 2010, and by the time it wound up I was an eleven-time winner.

With Aruna in Iceland, where the Vikings threw their 'bad women', in 2000.

Don't remember the joke, but bet it was funny. Between mouthfuls and laughs during a promotional event in Kolkata in 2001.

With Gelfand (l) and Aronian during the 2007 World Championship in Mexico.

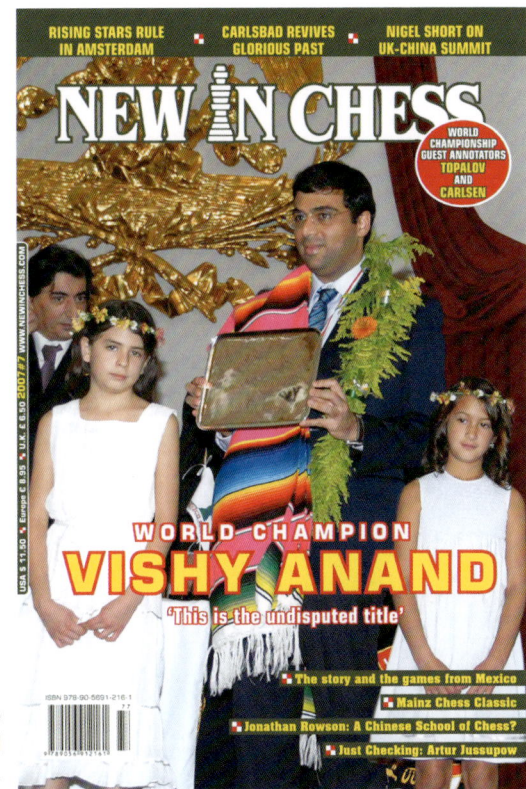

The cover of *New in Chess* magazine announcing my status as the undisputed World Champion after the Mexico win.

At the 2008 World Championship match in Bonn against Kramnik. Our friendship was put into cold storage during this one.

With the 2008 World Championship trophy in Bonn. I was a lot happier than I look.

Our eight-seater Mercedes Sprinter van being loaded with our suitcases in Bad Soden, Germany. My team and I were to embark on a 40-hour road journey through four countries to reach Sofia for the 2010 World Championship match.

My seconds and close friends (l-r) Nielsen, Christian Bossert, the Bulgarian special agent, Eric, Rustam, Hans-Walter Schmitt, Surya and Radek looking pleased in their Team Anand t-shirts in Sofia in 2010.

With the winner's trophy in Sofia, after a match that packed in every adventure I had never imagined I'd have.

You can't keep a chessboard beside me and expect that I'll look anywhere else. At the opening ceremony of the 2012 World Championship match in Moscow.

Gelfand and I have always been thick friends and playing each other for the 2012 World Championship title wasn't enough to snip that bond.

There's no greater joy than wearing a laurel wreath. After my win at the 2012 World Championship in Moscow.

Kramnik tells me that retired life keeps him busier than ever and he doesn't find the time to miss chess. I wonder if I can keep the game off my mind once I join him on the other side. With Kramnik at the board at the 2016 London Chess Classic. Wesley So, Anish Giri, Fabiano Caruana, Levon Aronian and Maxime Vachier-Lagrave looking on.

With my current trainer Grzegorz Gajewski in St Louis. A modern version of Ubilava, he has an uncanny eye for positions and moves on the board.

I could feel the sharp talons of this magnificent beauty despite the glove. At the 2017 World Rapid Championship in Riyadh.

The familiar feeling of being No 1. With Vladimir Fedoseev (right) and Ian Nepomniachtchi at the prize-giving ceremony in Riyadh in 2017.

With teammate Maxime Vachier-Lagrave (right) and chef Filip August Bendi (centre), after winning the 2019 Altibox Norway Chess cook-off for the second year in a row. Our gourmet dish of salmon with vegetables walked away with the top honors.

Gleeful after finishing on the winning side at St Louis 2019. Team Randy beat Team Rex 4–2 in Ultimate Moves, a Sinquefield Cup tradition of a fun six-round blitz team event, with the players alternating turns after five moves.

Akhil loves setting up the chessboard and knows how the pieces move. We learn so much from each other every day...